A LITTLE BOOK FOR

NEW HISTORIANS

WHY AND HOW TO STUDY HISTORY

ROBERT TRACY McKENZIE

IVP Academic

An imprint of InterVarsity Press
Downers Grove, Illinois

InterVarsity Press
P.O. Box 1400, Downers Grove, IL 60515-1426
ivpress.com
email@ivpress.com

InterVarsity Press® is the book-publishing division of InterVarsity Christian Fellowship/ USA®, a movement of students and faculty active on campus at hundreds of universities, colleges, and schools of nursing in the United States of America, and a member movement of the International Fellowship of Evangelical Students. For information about local and regional activities, visit intervarsity.org.

Cover design: Cindy Kiple
Interior design: Beth McGill

ISBN 978-0-8308-5346-5 (print)
ISBN 978-0-8308-7245-9 (digital)

Printed in the United States of America ∞

InterVarsity Press is committed to ecological stewardship and to the conservation of natural resources in all our operations. This book was printed using sustainably sourced paper.

Library of Congress Cataloging-in-Publication Data

A catalog record for this book is available from the Library of Congress.

P	20	19	18	17	16	15	14	13	12	11	10	9	8	7	6	5	4	3	2
Y	35	34	33	32	31	30	29	28	27	26	25	24	23	22	21				

"This slim volume will challenge everything you've learned about studying the past. Put names and dates to the side and buckle your seatbelts for a ride that engages your heart as much as your mind. New historians—and old—will benefit mightily from the wisdom of this little book."

Sam Wineburg, Margaret Jacks Professor of Education and (by courtesy) History, Stanford University

"This book makes an outstanding contribution—for students of history, readers of history, history classes in college or high school, and discussions of history in church groups. It explains clearly what historians do, how historical study can promote the right kind of intellectual discipline, and why history means so much for Christian faith. The book is as powerfully effective as it is accessibly succinct."

Mark Noll, author of *In the Beginning Was the Word: The Bible and American Public Life, 1492-1783*

"Beautifully written and thought provoking. Tracy McKenzie reminds us that history is so much more than knowledge about the past. He invites us to understand history as a Christian vocation; he equips us to develop historical habits of the mind, and he challenges us to be transformed by our historical consciousness. Just as history is foundational to Christian faith, McKenzie shows us that historical understanding is also foundational to being a faithful Christian. His book will enrich both the college and church classroom."

Beth Allison Barr, associate professor of history, associate dean of the graduate school at Baylor University

"If we take McKenzie's warnings about American 'present-tense culture' seriously and apply his lessons of history as the remembered past, the solutions for many of our contemporary racial problems would soon become clear. This book provides practical reflection and instruction on the development of historical thinking skills and growth of historical consciousness. I wish I had it when I was a new historian."

Robert Chao Romero, historian, UCLA Cesar E. Chavez Department of Chicana/o Studies

"This primer for new historians is full of Christian wisdom about the study of the past. Written by a seasoned veteran who has taught history majors for more than thirty years—in both secular and Christian academic institutions—it will instruct and transform you with profound historical thinking about the world in which we live and the people we should love. Read it and join the conversation!"

Douglas A. Sweeney, distinguished professor of church history and the history of Christian thought, Trinity Evangelical Divinity School

"More than a how-to for beginning history students, this book is a tonic for our times. When many on the left and right clamor for history instructors to teach 'what really happened,' McKenzie lays bare the prideful arrogance behind such a desire and reminds us what a mature historical consciousness can provide—a discerning eye for the situation in which one has to act. Brimming with valuable insights culled from decades of classroom instruction by a master teacher, reading this book is both an intellectual pleasure and a practicum for spiritual formation. One can hope that the author's awe and humility before the task of making sense of the past will rub off on everyone who takes up this book."

Lendol Calder, professor of history, Augustana College

"Tracy McKenzie writes that we are living in a 'present-tense culture.' This observation will come as no surprise to history teachers on the frontlines, whose students tend to see the study of history as an exercise in memorizing arcane facts and hence place little value on learning history. In this concise and accessible book, McKenzie shows a way out of the tyranny of the present, explaining both how and why to learn from the past. He shows how to develop habits of inquiry and reflection that allow engagement with the past as a life-changing moral inquiry rather than the dry recital of facts. The wisdom he offers for new historians can be fruitful for more experienced scholars as well. This small book should be on *every* historian's reading list."

Rob Sorensen, history department chair, The Bear Creek School

"In engaging and accessible prose, Tracy McKenzie provides an excellent introduction to the historian's craft for the undergraduate student—I know of none better. *A Little Book for New Historians* offers a compelling rationale for the study of history along with helpful practical guidelines on how to do so. But, above all, it challenges students to view history as an essential part of an education that endeavors to form mind and spirit in humane and holy ways. Deeply informed by Christian faith, this work summons the student to seek a 'heart of wisdom' through the careful investigation of the past."

Ronald K. Rittgers, Erich Markel Chair of German Reformation Studies, professor of history and theology, Valparaiso University

"*A Little Book for New Historians* is short on words and long on wisdom. In it, Tracy McKenzie proves once again to be a sure and reliable guide for Christian students and faculty on what it means to do history well and why it is worth it. Like the past itself, his work offers us lots of gifts to be received."

Richard Pointer, Westmont College

*For my colleagues and students
at Wheaton College*

■ ■ ■

CONTENTS

PART ONE

WHY STUDY HISTORY?

1

SO WHAT IS HISTORY ANYWAY?

*You keep using that word. I do not think
it means what you think it means.*

Inigo Montoya, *The Princess Bride*

■■■

OFTEN THE FAMILIAR WORDS mislead us most. When we come across a word that's entirely foreign to us, we hesitate to use it until we're sure what it means. But when it comes to words that we've known since childhood, we get reckless. Why stop to define terms that we've known since third grade? And so we muddle along, using words that we think we understand but haven't thought much about. Sometimes this works, and sometimes it gets us in trouble. *History* is a case in point.

It's not that *history* signifies such a complicated concept. The problem is that it signifies multiple distinct concepts. The editors

The Princess Bride, directed by Rob Reiner (Santa Monica, CA: MGM Home Entertainment, 2000). See www.imsdb.com/scripts/Princess-Bride,-The .html, accessed July 2, 2018.

of the *Oxford English Dictionary* have come up with twelve, believe it or not. We don't have to bother with all the nuanced shades of difference that the OED sets out, but we do have to be alert to one critical distinction that is absolutely foundational to everything that follows in this book.

In popular parlance, when we refer to *history* outside of an academic setting, we almost always mean "the past itself." We debate the best sports teams in history, question the checkered history of a political candidate, or celebrate John and Martha's long history together. No problem or confusion here; we all know what we mean. The danger comes when we carry that habit into the systematic, academic study of history. With apologies to popular culture, academic historians insist that history is *not* the past. They're not even close to the same. Coming to grips with the magnitude of the difference is the first essential step to thinking historically.

We're not just splitting hairs. The difference between the past and our knowledge of the past is so immense that it should stagger and humble us. The best illustration of the difference that I've come across is from one of the lesser known essays of C. S. Lewis. Lewis was a master at making esoteric truths understandable, and in his essay "Historicism" he crafted a marvelous metaphor for the past. Imagine that every single moment of "lived time" is like a drop of water, Lewis writes. If that were true, then it follows that "the past . . . in its reality, was a roaring cataract of billions upon billions of such moments: any one of them too complex to grasp in its entirety, and the aggregate beyond all imagination."

What a word picture! By inviting us to imagine ourselves near the base of a deafening waterfall, Lewis helps us to glimpse the nearly limitless scope of the past. As you read his words, imagine standing by the water's edge with your arm outstretched, a Dixie cup in hand. If that wall of water plummeting downward is analogous to "the past" in its near-infinite totality, then the drops that you capture in your paper cup represent *history*, i.e., all that we can claim to recall and comprehend of those "billions upon billions" of moments. As Lewis recognized, the difference between history and the past "is not a question of [our] failing to know everything: it is a question (at least as regards quantity) of knowing next door to nothing." Try as we may, we can catch but a fraction of that crashing cataract; the rest "falls off the world into total oblivion."[1]

If reminding ourselves of the disparity between history and the past is the first step to thinking historically, it is also a crucial part of thinking Christianly while thinking historically. After three decades in the academy, I'm still wrestling with what it means to

> IF THAT WALL OF WATER PLUMMETING DOWNWARD IS ANALOGOUS TO "THE PAST," THEN THE DROPS THAT YOU CAPTURE IN YOUR PAPER CUP REPRESENT *HISTORY*.

think Christianly as a historian, but here are two things I think it has to include: awe and humility. When it comes to history, thinking Christianly should inspire us with awe when we recall God's omniscient comprehension of the near-infinite past. Our

---

[1]C. S. Lewis, "Historicism," in *Christian Reflections*, ed. Walter Hooper (Grand Rapids: Eerdmans, 1967), 107.

Lord "has numbered the hairs of our heads as well as the days of princes and kings."[2]

But thinking Christianly should also lead us to humility when we remind ourselves, following Lewis, that in our human finiteness, our knowledge of the past is, by comparison, "next door to nothing." When we equate history with the past, we exaggerate our capacity to know, minimize the wonder of divine omniscience, and unwittingly attempt to rob God of a measure of his glory. For the Christian historian, calling to mind the vast difference between history and the past can be a kind of spiritual discipline, a way of promoting humility and awe by reminding ourselves that God is God and we are not.

So *history* is not the entirety of the past and there are important reasons to remember that. Fair enough. But how then are we to define it? (That Dixie cup analogy is a bit unwieldy.) The truth is that academic historians don't agree on a single, "official" definition, but whatever definition they embrace, it always preserves this fundamental distinction between history and the past. You'll find some who define *history* as "the *recreation* of the past," others who speak of it as "the *analysis* or *interpretation* of the past," or even as "a never-ending *argument* about the past." Actually, it's all of these things. The definition I think is best— and the one we'll build on in the rest of this chapter—is that *history* is "the *remembered* past," a phrase that I borrow from Christian historian John Lukacs.[3]

---

[2]Arthur S. Link, "The Historian's Vocation," *Theology Today* 19 (1962/1963): 86.
[3]Mark G. Malvasi and Jeffrey O. Nelson, eds., *Remembered Past: John Lukacs on History, Historians, and Historical Knowledge* (Wilmington, DE: ISI Books, 2005), 4-5, italics added.

The power of this pithy definition is remarkable. Once we begin to think consciously of historical knowledge as a form of memory, the analogy unlocks all manner of truths about what history is and what historians do.

ONCE WE BEGIN TO THINK CONSCIOUSLY OF HISTORICAL KNOWLEDGE AS A FORM OF MEMORY, THE ANALOGY UNLOCKS ALL MANNER OF TRUTHS ABOUT WHAT HISTORY IS AND WHAT HISTORIANS DO.

Think for a few moments about memory. What function does it serve in our lives? What traits do you associate with it? When I posed these questions to my students last semester, their answers were spot on. On the one hand, they recognized the critical role that memory plays for all of us. "Memory is crucial to our sense of personal identity," one student commented. "Without it we would be unable to function," observed another.

But if the function of memory is vital, the traits of memory give us pause. My students observed that we forget most of what happens to us. What we do remember we often remember inaccurately, frequently selectively, sometimes self-servingly. Our memories regularly change over time, furthermore, and it is next to impossible to find two people who remember the same event in precisely the same way.

If history is the remembered past, how might these attributes of memory help us in thinking about history? I can think of at least four related conclusions that follow. First, *history is foundational to our sense of identity*. It's a truism that our personal memories are vital to our sense of self. In like manner, history can speak both to the question "Who am I?" as well as to the broader question "Who are we?" We are historical beings and we cannot survive without historical knowledge.

Second, just as we all have memories, it's equally true that *we all know some history*, even if we think otherwise. We tend to equate historical knowledge with the dates and names in history books—the kind of information that we happily forget once we've taken the final exam. But when we think of history as the remembered past, we see how silly it is to claim that we don't know any. We all have a sense of our personal history, for starters. What Lukacs describes as "the inevitable presence of the past in our lives" is one of the defining attributes of our humanity.[4]

Third, *we are all already historians*, and that's true whether we've ever darkened the door of an archive or worn a tweed jacket with elbow patches. The title of this book suggests that it is pitched for "*new* historians," but that doesn't really describe you unless you've only just begun to have memories. At the heart of the historian's pursuit is drawing on knowledge of the past in order to understand the present and act effectively in the future. None of us can survive without doing this daily. This means that "history is something we all do," as historian Margaret MacMillan observes, "even if, like the man who discovered he was writing prose, we do not always realize it."[5]

This understanding of history as the remembered past contradicts the common perception of history as an esoteric branch of knowledge belonging exclusively to academic

---

[4]Malvasi and Nelson, *Remembered Past*, 4.
[5]Margaret MacMillan, *Dangerous Games: The Uses and Abuses of History* (New York: Modern Library, 2010), ix.

specialists. (That's a perception that we academic historians have too often fostered, by the way.) But if we are all already historians who know some history, *it doesn't follow that we are automatically equipped to remember the past accurately and wisely*. The analogy between history and memory points us toward this final conclusion as well. Remember how faulty memory can be?

There is an old Asian proverb to the effect that the palest ink is more reliable than the strongest memory.[6] Academic historians insist that the best history is memory corroborated by evidence, and that the astute historian uses every kind of evidence available to remember the past as accurately as possible. There is something of a paradox here, if you'll notice it. *History* may be "something we all do," but

> THE ASTUTE HISTORIAN USES EVERY KIND OF EVIDENCE AVAILABLE TO REMEMBER THE PAST AS ACCURATELY AS POSSIBLE.

sound *historical thinking* is something we have to work at. As one influential work puts it, thinking historically is an "unnatural act."[7]

This is why academic historians often use the term history to refer not only to a branch of knowledge but also to an intellectual

---

[6]"The Palest Ink Is Better Than the Best Memory," Chinese Idioms—Chengyu, Standard Mandarin Chinese Pronunciation, accessed October 5, 2018, www.standardmandarin.com/idiom/the-palest-ink-is-better-than-the-best-memory-idiom.

[7]Sam Wineburg, *Historical Thinking and Other Unnatural Acts: Charting the Future of Teaching the Past* (Philadelphia: Temple University Press, 2001).

discipline in which the mind is trained to analyze historical evidence and build sound historical arguments. Much of the second half of this book will explore the habits of mind that sharpen our historical thinking and enhance our capacity to remember the past rightly. But before we get there, we need to remind ourselves why remembering rightly is so important.

2

OUR "PRESENT-TENSE CULTURE"

■ ■ ■

SO WHY SHOULD WE CARE about the past in the first place? The rest of part one of this book is devoted to just that question, but before we go down that road, I want to warn you: I am going to be encouraging you to engage in a pursuit that, for Americans in the twenty-first century, is a highly countercultural, even radical act.

The late social critic Christopher Hitchens nailed it when he observed that Americans inhabit a "present-tense culture."[1] We live in a society in which thinking deeply about the past is rare and becoming ever more so. In the 1970s about 5 percent of undergraduates across the country majored in history; today about 1 percent do so. We still pay lip service to the teaching of history in our public schools, but middle school and high school students across America have a less than one-in-five chance of learning history from a teacher who actually majored in history in college. Anybody can teach history, after all, since it (supposedly) involves little more than the memorization of names and dates.

---

[1]Christopher Hitchens, "Good-Bye to All That: Why Americans Are Not Taught History," *Harpers*, November 1998, 37.

I haven't done a scientific survey, but my sense is that the majority of Americans fall into one of two groups in their thinking about the importance of the past. The first group sees no value in history at all. Its members are the disciples of the late Henry Ford (although they don't know enough history to realize it). The early twentieth-century automobile tycoon—and for a time, the richest man in the world—once famously lectured Americans on the irrelevance of the past. "History is more or less bunk," Ford expostulated. "It's tradition. We don't want tradition. We want to live in the present, and the only history that is worth a tinker's damn is the history we make today."[2]

(Over the years I often put quotes about the value of history on my course syllabi, and believe it or not, I often include this one, though usually paired with another I like better: "You can design a decent car and still believe something utterly stupid."—Tracy McKenzie.)

The second group, implicitly at least, thinks of history as a source of entertainment. Not surprisingly, many in this category learn their history from the entertainment industry itself. They base their knowledge of the past on "docudramas" and feature films "based on a true story"—an advertising euphemism for "mostly, but not entirely, made up." To cite one example, not long after the re-lease of the movie *Forrest Gump*, a detailed field study of high school students found that nearly two-thirds of those surveyed based their understanding of the Vietnam War on that fanciful film. For many Americans, "Hollywood history is the only history."[3]

---

[2]Mike Wallace, *Mickey Mouse History and Other Essays on American Memory* (Philadelphia: Temple University Press, 1996), 9.

[3]Sam Wineburg, Susan Mosborg, and Dan Porat, "What Can 'Forrest Gump' Tell Us About Students' Historical Understanding?," *Social*

Members of this second group may also think of history as a vast repository of amusing anecdotes and oddities—the kind of trivia that comes in handy if you're playing *Jeopardy*. ("I'll take History for $200, Alex.") They prefer their history to read like the *National Enquirer*—full of UFOs, ancient aliens, and the paranormal. This is the audience that the "History" Channel targets with documentaries on Bigfoot, zombies, and "Ghosts in the White House." Personally, I'll take Henry Ford over the History Channel any day. It seems less arrogant to dismiss the past entirely than to trivialize it so grotesquely.

What's bizarre about this is that we are creatures who live *in time*. By necessity, we make sense of our lives *retrospectively*. As Søren Kierkegaard put it, "We live forward, but we can only think backward."[4] And yet Americans are happily "stranded in the present," as historian Margaret Bendroth points out.[5]

> We live forward, but we can only think backward.
>
> Søren Kierkegaard

Education 65 (2001): 55; Mark Carnes, ed., *Past Imperfect: History According to the Movies* (New York: Henry Holt, 1995), 9.

[4] Quoted in John Lukacs, *A Student's Guide to the Study of History* (Wilmington, DE: ISI Books, 2000), 47.

[5] Margaret Bendroth, *The Spiritual Practice of Remembering* (Grand Rapids: Eerdmans, 2013), chap. 1. Bendroth borrows the phrase "stranded in the present" from Peter Fritzsche, *Stranded in the Present: Modern Time and the Melancholy of History* (Cambridge, MA: Harvard University Press, 2004), while imparting to it a decidedly different meaning.

I love the word picture embedded in that phrase. By one estimate, 93 percent of all the human beings who have ever drawn breath on earth are no longer living, while we who are still breathing live cut off from them, seemingly unwilling to listen to or learn from the vast majority of the human race. By writing that we are "stranded," Bendroth hints at the cost that comes with severing ourselves from the past. But the truth is we're not really castaways, marooned against our will and longing to be rescued so that we can reconnect with those who have gone before us. It's more accurate to say that we live in self-imposed exile, content with the soul-impoverishing isolation that comes with it. We're not just ignorant of the past, in other words. We're contemptuous of it. *USA* might as well stand for "United States of Amnesia."[6]

So why is this? How are we to explain it? The answer is surely complicated, but there are some likely culprits. As you consider them, note that I'm trying to understand a present-day pattern—contemporary Americans' blinkered present mindedness—by situating it in a larger historical context. This, in a nutshell, is one of the most important reasons we must study the past: it offers a vantage point from which to see our own world with new eyes.

So here are some possibilities. First, as numerous historians have pointed out, as Americans, we remember our nation's birth as a radical rupture with the past. Our Founding Fathers, we like to say, turned their backs on the Old World and brought something entirely new into being: a "new order of the ages" as those

---

[6]Carnes, *Past Imperfect*, 9.

strange Latin words (*novus ordo seclorum*) declare on the back of our dollar bills. We still refer to the United States as an "experiment," and an awful lot of Americans are convinced that our country is "exceptional." This doesn't leave much room for gaining wisdom from the stories of other times and places. By this way of thinking, the past becomes primarily a catalog of errors to avoid.

By the middle of the nineteenth century, the conviction that all but the most recent past was irrelevant had become an American dogma. "We are the great nation of futurity," trumpeted the prominent journalist John O'Sullivan, popularizer of the catch phrase "manifest destiny." "Our national birth was the beginning of a new history . . . which separates us from the past and connects us with the future only," O'Sullivan informed readers of the *Democratic Review*. "We have no interest in the scenes of antiquity, only as lessons of avoidance of nearly all their examples. The expansive future is our arena." As assertions go, it was arrogant, ignorant, anti-intellectual—and wildly popular.[7]

Second, there is reason to believe that the same forces that have promoted democracy and individualism in American culture have also helped to sever our ties to the past. Shortly before O'Sullivan proclaimed history's irrelevance to the United States, Frenchman Alexis de Tocqueville posited that one of the general consequences of the rise of democracy would be an increasing present mindedness. In his classic *Democracy in*

---

[7]John L. O'Sullivan, "The Great Nation of Futurity," *The United States Democratic Review* 6, no. 23 (1839): 426-27.

America, Tocqueville theorized that as a society becomes more democratic, "the bond that ties generation to generation is loosened or broken. People easily lose track of the ideas of their ancestors or cease to care about them." Generalizing further, Tocqueville postulated that "democratic peoples . . . care little about what happened in Rome or Athens. . . . What they ask to be shown is a picture of the present."[8] This sounds a lot like Henry Ford.

> Democratic peoples . . . care little about what happened in Rome or Athens. . . . What they ask to be shown is a picture of the present.
>
> Alexis de Tocqueville

A third factor, I suspect, is technological. Two centuries ago, most Americans, like most humans generally, lived lives not that different from their parents' and grandparents.' They would have earned their bread in more or less the same fashion, and their life expectancy, diet, income, and overall material standard of well-being would have been more or less comparable as well. Beginning near the turn of the nineteenth century, however, rapid technological change began to explode these patterns of continuity across much of the United States and western Europe. Because relentless technological change is now like the air we

---

[8]Alexis de Tocqueville, *Democracy in America*, trans. Arthur Goldhammer (New York: Penguin Random House, 2004), 484, 564.

breathe, we're often blind to the ways that it conditions us to see the world.

Certainly one of its effects has been to teach us to view anything from the past as inferior. Equating technological change with progress, we conclude that all previous generations have been backward, which in turn undermines any argument for taking the past seriously. As Bendroth notes, one of the easiest ways to dismiss historical figures is simply to imagine how lost they would be in the present. As I write this, a popular cable TV company pitches its services by likening consumers without the latest technology to quaint nineteenth-century settlers who churn their own butter and spin their own yarn. Looking for a symbol to represent ignorance and backwardness? No problem. The past is full of them.

The relentless movement that has characterized Americans for much of the past two centuries surely also reinforces our present mindedness. This was driven home to me during a recent visit with my father-in-law in his home in the rural South. Living in the same small farming community where he was born, Hunter sees reminders of his past in every direction. The church where his family worshipped as he was growing up (established in the 1830s) is a mile away. The school that his friends and neighbors attended and where his mother taught is just down the road. His best friend from childhood lives across the highway. As we drive to dinner, he tells me who is buried in the cemetery off the road, explains who used to own the abandoned store we just passed, points out the house where the president of the senior class of 1956 still lives.

In Hunter's world, so different from my own, the past is a tangible frame of reference for the present. In contrast, most of us live in communities with revolving doors—ever shifting conglomerations of strangers—with the result that we have lost the sense of physical connection with a personal past. The generations that have gone before us become abstractions. It becomes easier to ridicule them and, eventually, to ignore them.

Finally, it is likely that the influence of Protestant Christianity on American culture has also strengthened our present mindedness. If you're a Protestant, as I am, you've been trained to be skeptical of most of church history. As heirs of the Protestant Reformation, we're suspicious of tradition and tend to think of the millennium and a half between the time of the apostles and the arrival of Martin Luther as an enormous black hole. But even that's probably too generous. American evangelicals

> **WE HAVE LOST THE SENSE OF PHYSICAL CONNECTION WITH A PERSONAL PAST. THE GENERATIONS THAT HAVE GONE BEFORE US BECOME ABSTRACTIONS.**

often think of church history as really starting with Billy Graham (or even Rick Warren or Joel Osteen). The growth of nondenominational churches in recent decades has only heightened this sense of disjuncture with the past. These congregations have no ties to larger denominations and a brief lifespan of their own, and the Christians who affiliate with such churches, like Americans more generally, find it hard to think of themselves as part of a story that began long before they arrived on the scene.

Yes, we live in a present-tense culture. But so what? Henry Ford was fine with that, and he was a bazillionaire. What's the argument for thinking he was wrong?

3

PRACTICAL REWARDS

■ ■ ■

ABOUT THE SAME TIME that Ford was getting started on his famous Model T, a Harvard philosopher named George Santayana was putting the finishing touches on his own labor of love, a magnum opus to be titled *The Life of Reason: The Stages of Human Progress*. This was good news for the minority of Americans who denied that history was "bunk," who wanted to believe that the past is important and that our lives are impoverished by ignoring it. It's a commentary on the pervasive present mindedness of American society, however, that even those who want to be champions of history often aren't sure how to go about it. And it's surely one of the great ironies of history that the single most quoted aphorism in defense of history came from the pen of a man who wasn't thinking about history at all.

Buried on page 284 of volume one of this five-volume, seventeen hundred-page treatise, we find the following: "Those who cannot remember the past are condemned to repeat it." Poor Santayana. A respected scholar a century ago and author of more than two dozen works on philosophy, we remember him today, if we remember him at all, for this single sentence wrenched out of context from his extensive writings and tortured to mean something he never intended.

In context, Santayana was explaining a common sense principle, namely that the acquisition of knowledge is incremental. If at the end of every day we were to forget everything that we had ever known, the limits of our knowledge would never move beyond what we could acquire from scratch in the span of twenty-four hours. We would be perpetually like newborn babies, which was precisely Santayana's point. "When experience is not retained," he wrote, "infancy is perpetual." His very next sentence—"those who cannot remember the past are condemned to repeat it"—was a fanciful way of expressing this truism.[1]

In sum, Santayana the philosopher was making a general statement about the nature of knowledge. By taking his axiom out of context, we remember him as a historian forging an axiom about the nature of the past and the value of history. Politicians and pundits love the quote. It sounds profound, and it makes history into a storehouse of simple lessons that we ignore at our peril: "Never get involved in a land war in Asia." "Never go up against a Sicilian when death is on the line," and so on.[2] (Not coincidentally, these obvious "lessons" almost always vindicate our predetermined agendas, and they're rarely obvious at all to those who don't already agree with us.)

---

[1] George Santayana, *The Life of Reason, or the Phases of Human Progress* (New York: Charles Scribner's Sons, 1905), 1:284.

[2] *The Princess Bride*, directed by Rob Reiner (Santa Monica, CA: MGM Home Entertainment, 2000). See the Internet Movie Script Database, imsdb.com/scripts/Princess-Bride,-The.html.

To academic historians, the lessons-of-history approach violates one of the cardinal principles guiding our study of the past: *History is complicated.* (Because I use the phrase so regularly in the classroom, my daughter has suggested that "It's complicated" would be a fitting epitaph for my tombstone.) Human behavior is complex. The past is almost infinitely vast. The echoes and shadows of human behavior that survive in the form of historical evidence are always woefully incomplete. Establishing definitive chains of cause and effect is next to impossible.

As we engage this complexity—really come to feel the weight of it—we become reflexively leery of simplistic historical lessons supposedly applicable in all times and places. All serious historians are convinced that knowledge of the past is key to understanding the present. But an appreciation of historical complexity teaches us to reject the mechanistic, deterministic view of the past that "condemned to repeat it," if taken literally, requires of us. History equips us not to predict the future but to meet it more wisely.

> **HISTORY EQUIPS US NOT TO PREDICT THE FUTURE BUT TO MEET IT MORE WISELY.**

(This, by the way, also explains why no serious historian should give credence to the overworked phrase "the wrong side of history," an increasingly common putdown among politicians and political commentators. When we dismiss someone with whom we disagree as being on "the wrong side of history," we're essentially saying that we've peered into our crystal balls and seen that, in the long run, the majority agrees with *us.* Setting aside the dubious proposition that majority opinion bears any correlation with moral truth, declarations about the wrong and right "side of history" are, in their essence, predictions of the future. Mature historians don't do that.)

As a Christian historian, I find further reason to reject Santayana's supposed observation about history repeating itself. Our misreading of Santayana makes his dictum an echo of the ancient Greek historian Thucydides, who hoped that his *History of the Peloponnesian War* would be read by those who "wish to have a clear view both of the events which have happened and of those which will some day . . . happen again in the same or a similar way."[3] One of the consequences of the spread of Christianity was to challenge this ancient, pagan view of human history as cyclical. Because Christians recognize creation, fall, redemption, and consummation as central to the human story, we view it not as cyclical but as linear. In C. S. Lewis's apt phrase, we're studying a "story with a divine plot"—an unfolding, meaningful movement toward a divinely appointed culmination.[4]

Santayana's dictum sounds profound, but if academic historians don't believe it and Christians should heartily reject it, we're clearly in need of a better reason to study history. Thankfully, there are many. There are so many, in fact, that it will take the rest of the first half of this book even to scratch the surface.

Let's start with some basic categories. Regardless of the field of study, any academic pursuit worthy of your time and energy should lead to three kinds of change in your life: change in your

---

[3]Thucydides, *History of the Peloponnesian War*, trans. Charles F. Smith (Cambridge, MA: Harvard University Press, 1935), 41.
[4]C. S. Lewis, *The Discarded Image* (Cambridge: Cambridge University Press, 1964), 176.

knowledge, your intellect, and your consciousness—in what you know, how you think, and who you are. As someone poised to begin the serious study of history, this means that you should aspire to acquire historical knowledge, develop historical thinking skills, and grow in historical consciousness. Let's consider each in turn.

At its most basic, *historical knowledge* is simply knowledge about the past, but we're better served by breaking it into its two component parts: historical information and historical understanding. By *historical information*, I simply mean historical facts, those little, individual bits of information about the past that have a way of showing up as answers on multiple-choice exams. 1066. Neil Armstrong. The Diet of Worms. The Second Punic War. Eli Whitney. 1492. Schlieffen Plan. Henry V. The Ming Dynasty. Congress of Vienna. Manhattan Project. Triangular trade.

Ask the typical person on the street what sets a professional historian apart, and they'll almost always answer with this kind of information in mind. They assume that trained historians simply know more stuff about the past than other folks—our heads are crammed with names and dates and arcane facts about battles and kings. I remember confessing to a new acquaintance at church that my memory was poor, and she immediately replied, "Then how in the world can you be a historian?" To this individual, as to so many of us, history is simply a body of information that you memorize.

How boring.

I'm going to say something that may surprise you to hear a history professor say, but I also hope you'll find it freeing: by themselves, historical facts are not just mind numbing. They're meaningless. Wrench a historical fact from its context and it instantly becomes insignificant. ("No context, no meaning," I like to say.) Accurate information about the past is invaluable to the historian, but it is valuable as a means to an end, not as an end in itself. What we're really after is *historical understanding*.

When I think of historical understanding, my mind goes to an old *New Yorker* cartoon that I used to have on my office door. It centers on a stereotypical academic egghead— old, shriveled, balding, wearing

> BY THEMSELVES, HISTORICAL FACTS ARE NOT JUST MIND NUMBING. THEY'RE MEANINGLESS.

glasses that look like the bottom of old Coke bottles. He is hunched over his desk, peering into a musty volume slightly smaller than a Mini Cooper and surrounded by floor-to-ceiling book shelves crammed with equally enormous tomes. Then in a moment of feverish ecstasy he looks up from his reading and exclaims, "For a minute there it suddenly all made sense!"

It's never *all* going to make sense, but that's what we're striving for. The quest for historical understanding is the quest *to make sense of the past*. Because historical facts are crucial to that task, professional historians typically spend a great deal of time poring over historical evidence: from written records such as diaries, correspondence, newspapers, legal records, census books, and muster rolls to a host of physical artifacts ranging from art work to architecture to archaeological remains. But the real work of the historian is to figure out what the historical evidence that we discover actually means. This is where *historical thinking skills* come in.

Clichés aside, the facts never "speak for themselves." Historical information only becomes significant as historians piece it together into intelligible patterns. We build historical understanding by fitting the facts that we glean from the evidence into a coherent, persuasive story about the past that is as true to past reality as we can make it. This is no simple undertaking. It requires our best powers of analysis and logical argument. We must train our minds to ways of thinking and knowing that are unnatural and yet indispensable to understanding the past on its own terms.

BUILDING HISTORICAL UNDERSTANDING BY FITTING FACTS INTO A COHERENT, PERSUASIVE STORY ABOUT THE PAST IS NO SIMPLE UNDERTAKING.

The practical benefits of historical understanding and historical thinking skills are enormous. When I meet with parents at our beginning-of-the-year academic fair, I always start with history's most material rewards. This is a concession to our cultural climate. We live in a world that is pragmatic as well as present minded. From local school boards to state legislatures to the President of the United States, we're told to think of education in materialistic, instrumental terms. Its primary purpose is not to broaden the mind and ennoble the spirit, but to help us land a job, increase our earning potential, and make the United States more competitive in global markets.

Despite a growing mountain of evidence to the contrary, the majority of Americans are convinced that the serious study of the liberal arts is a waste of time and money, or at the very least a luxury that we can't afford. And so I steel myself for the inevitable question, asked over and over by nervous parents trying to steer their idealistic sons and daughters across the gym toward the science and engineering tables. "What can you do with history except teach?" they ask politely. My ready answer—met with polite disbelief—is "pretty much anything."

Over three decades of working with history majors, I'd estimate that less than one in five have gone on to become history teachers or to work in closely related fields such as museum studies, archive management, or historical preservation. The vast majority have taken different paths: in banking, financial planning, and insurance; in library science and computer science; in the national park service or the foreign service; in film production, law enforcement, and public affairs; in medicine, the ministry, or the military. Others are earning their bread as journalists, attorneys, firefighters, chefs, pilots, social workers, urban planners, and community organizers.

The explanation for this should be obvious. The academic study of history is less a gateway to a particular occupation than a stepping stone to lifelong learning. Yet its practical benefits include an array of intellectual skills that are integral to any number of occupations. These include the ability to read closely, think analytically, argue logically, and communicate persuasively. The evidence that these are among the traits that employers most highly value is overwhelming. A recent survey of employers found that 93 percent agreed that "a demonstrated capacity to think critically, communicate clearly, and solve complex problems is more important than [a job candi-date's] major."[5]

But I refuse to reduce history's practical rewards solely to the question of earnings potential. History's civic benefits are also invaluable. At its best, rigorous historical study equips us to be informed, responsible citizens. We live in a society that, for all its present mindedness, still appeals to the past in moments of crisis. Debates over welfare, affirmative action, voting rights, foreign policy, same-sex marriage, and religious freedom regu-larly involve appeals to historical evidence. I began this book in the midst of a presidential election cycle, against a backdrop of claims and counterclaims about the historical roots of the "party of Lincoln," about the original intent of the Second Amendment, about the past successes and failures of US immigration policy, and about the validity of Alexis de Tocqueville's supposed claim that "America is great because America is good." (Tocqueville actually never said anything of the kind.)

Historical understanding helps us to discern the strengths and flaws in political rhetoric. The critical thinking skills that historical study promotes also help us to evaluate policy proposals, avoid groupthink, and bring reason to public dia-logue. Most important, because the study of history requires that we view the world from others' perspectives, it enhances our capacity for empathy. Few qualities are more essential to the flourishing of a pluralistic democracy.

---

[5]Zach Budryk, "More Than a Major," *Inside Higher Ed*, April 10, 2013, insidehighered.com/news/2013/04/10/survey-finds-business-executives -arent-focused-majors-those-they-hire.

As valuable as these benefits are, the highest goal of historical study is neither historical knowledge, nor historical thinking skills, but *historical consciousness*. Historical consciousness is so valuable—and so rare—that we'll devote all of the next chapter to discussing it.

> HISTORICAL STUDY CHANGES WHAT WE KNOW, HOW WE THINK, AND WHO WE ARE.

4

TRANSFORMATION

■■■

IN OUR PRAGMATIC PREOCCUPATION with the bottom line, Americans have gradually forgotten the difference between vocational training and education. Both are important. Vocational training is valuable because we need to make a living, and when we're proficient in our work we bless others as well. But you can make a comfortable living and be good at your job without ever being educated in the deepest sense. At its fullest, education entails more than the accumulation of knowledge and the development of skills. The term descends from two Latin roots: *educare*, which means to "train" or "lead," but also *educere*, which means "to draw out."[1] That etymology reminds us that authentic education always involves what one writer calls "inner work."[2] Vocational training prepares us for a job. Education changes who we are.

This is why, of all the potential benefits of studying history, the development of historical consciousness is the most truly

---

[1] Randall V. Bass and J. W. Good, "Educare and Educere: Is a Balance Possible in the Educational System?," *Educational Forum* 68 (2004): 161-68.
[2] E. F. Schumacher, *A Guide for the Perplexed* (New York: Harper & Row, 1977), 85.

educational. Writing in the middle of the previous century, Cambridge historian Herbert Butterfield maintained that historical knowledge is most valuable when it is "transmuted into a deeper wisdom that melts into the rest of experience and is incorporated in the fabric of the mind itself."[3] Historical consciousness isn't

> HISTORICAL CONSCIOUSNESS ISN'T INFORMATION WE POSSESS OR A SKILL THAT WE PRACTICE. IT'S A *MINDSET* THAT CHANGES HOW WE SEE BOTH OURSELVES AND THE WORLD.

information we possess or a skill that we practice. It's a *mindset* that changes how we see both ourselves and the world.

Historical consciousness is born with *the realization that we are historical beings*. As John Lukacs summarizes, "Human existence is historical existence." Not only is our identity rooted in the past, but our very survival depends on memory of the past. As a guide to living, it's all that we have. "The present is no more than an illusion," Lukacs explains, "a moment that is already past in an instant. . . . And what we know about the future is nothing else than our projection of our past knowledge into it."[4]

But there's much more to historical consciousness than this. It's not just that we all depend in some way on knowledge of the past. To say that we are historical beings is also to acknowledge *the continued presence of the past in our lives*. William Faulkner

---

[3]Herbert Butterfield, *History and Human Relations* (London: Collins, 1951), 173.
[4]John Lukacs, *The Remembered Past* (Wilmington, DE: ISI Books, 2005), 2; Lukacs, *A Student's Guide to the Study of History* (Wilmington, DE: ISI Books, 2000), 3.

is famous for writing that "the past is never dead. It's not even past."[5] More poetically, in *Intruder in the Dust*, one of Faulkner's characters explains, "It's all *now* you see. Yesterday won't be over until tomorrow and tomorrow began ten thousand years ago."[6] Faulkner was speaking figuratively, not literally. The actual past *is* gone. (Remember C. S. Lewis's "roaring cataract" that "falls off the world into total oblivion.") But the *power* of the past lives on. Its influence is ever with us, ever a part of us, shaping who we are, what we notice, how we see.

> People from the past were not the only ones operating within a cultural context—we have one, too. Just like them we cannot imagine life any other way than it is: everyone assumes that 'what is' is what was meant to be.
>
> Margaret Bendroth

This is why, as you develop as a historian, one of the habits of mind you will acquire is the practice of reflexively situating individuals from the past in a larger historical context. If there is a single truth that inspires the serious study of history, it's Faulkner's conviction that we can never fully understand the present apart from the past. We take it as an axiom that we gain valuable insight into the human condition by positioning the lives of men and women in the larger flow of human experience over time. The person who has developed historical consciousness comes

---

[5]William Faulkner, *Requiem for a Nun* (New York: Random House, 1950), 92.
[6]William Faulkner, *Intruder in the Dust* (New York: Random House, 1948), 194.

to see this instinctively. She would never try to understand individuals from the past in a vacuum, severed from the historical context that framed and informed their lives.

But the person with true historical consciousness doesn't only apply this sensitivity to figures from the past. *Our* lives are similarly affected by what has gone before us. To quote Margaret Bendroth again, "People from the past were not the only ones operating within a cultural context—we have one, too. Just like them we cannot imagine life any other way than it is: everyone assumes that 'what is' is what was meant to be."[7]

This can be a sobering self-discovery. We're not nearly as autonomous as we would like to think. Like the historical figures we encounter, *we also live in time.* Like them, we were born into historical contexts that matter, settings that inform, influence, shape, and constrain who we become and how we see the world around us. And like them, we are often only dimly aware of the forces, large and small, that have such a profound impact on our lives.

Over two centuries ago, the British poet and essayist Samuel Taylor Coleridge captured this final truth with a memorable word picture. In the paragraph below, Coleridge ridicules our tendency to see a philosophy or worldview (what he refers to as "speculation and theory") as something far removed from daily living. His prose is hard going, but it handsomely repays our effort.

> In every state, not wholly barbarous, a philosophy, good or bad,
> there must be. However slightingly it may be the fashion to talk
> of speculation and theory, as opposed (sillily and nonsensically

---

[7]Margaret Bendroth, *The Spiritual Practice of Remembering* (Grand Rapids: Eerdmans, 2013), 49.

opposed) to practice, it would not be difficult to prove, that such
as is the existing spirit of speculation, during any given period,
such will be the spirit and tone of the religion, legislation, and
morals, nay, even of the fine arts, the manners, and the fashions.
Nor is this the less true, because the great majority of men live
like bats, but in twilight, and know and feel the philosophy of
their age only by its reflections and refractions.[8]

In these three complex sentences Coleridge makes three
crucial observations. First, *every* time and place is characterized
by a predominant philosophy or way of looking at the world. (This
might include answers to questions like, where do we come from?
Why are we here? What are the basic traits of human nature?
What should be the basis of our moral decisions? What is the ideal
function and structure of society?) Second, the conventional as-
sumptions that prevail in a particular place and time are hardly
limited to formal academic theorizing ("speculation"). Their spirit
is everywhere: in law and literature, art and architecture, music
and fashion, and every other facet of popular culture. Third and
most sobering, the philosophy of our time and place is something
that most of us will absorb subconsciously rather than contemplate systematically. Coleridge's word picture is powerful. Like
bats guided by sound waves bouncing off of the terrain around
them, we too can be guided by forces that we feel more than see.

One of the best ways to guard against such cultural blindness
is to make regular forays into the past. Here it is useful to think
of history not only as a form of memory, but also as a kind of

---

[8]Samuel Taylor Coleridge, *Essays on His Own Times, Forming a Second Series
of the Friend* (London: William Pickering, 1850), 708-9.

mirror that enables us to see ourselves more clearly. As Coleridge reminds us, one of the great paradoxes of life is that we're often unaware of the cultural values that influence us most deeply. This is because we see them as "natural," and what we see as natural we eventually cease to see at all. One of the great benefits of studying history is its potential to remind us that the way things are now is not the way they've always been. In the process, the aspects of our worldview that we take for granted—ways of thinking and being that are literally invisible to us—can sometimes come into focus.

I learned this anew a decade ago when I decided to write a book on the way that Americans have remembered the Pilgrims' 1621 celebration of "the First Thanksgiving." Like just about everyone else I know, I hadn't really studied the Pilgrims since elementary school. As I began to study them seriously, they were gradually transformed in my mind's eye. The cardboard caricatures I had

> STUDYING HISTORY REMINDS US THAT THE WAY THINGS ARE NOW IS NOT THE WAY THEY'VE ALWAYS BEEN.

carried around since third grade evolved into complicated three-dimensional beings whose behavior and beliefs were alternately familiar and bizarre.

For example, one of the surprising things that I learned about the Pilgrims is that they didn't believe in church marriage. Their reasoning was straightforward. As devout Puritans, they believed that both the Catholic Church and, to a lesser degree, the Church of England, had ambitiously expanded the power of the Church by giving the clergy unscriptural authority. With regard to marriage, they noted that Scripture never explicitly charges pastors with the responsibility of sacralizing the union of husbands and wives. Observing that marriage applied to "Gentiles" as well as Christians, they concluded that it is a *civil* rite. Their longtime governor, William Bradford, denounced the Catholic and Anglican practice of requiring church marriages as an example of "popish" aggrandizement. A truly devout Puritan, Bradford taught, would never submit to be married by a clergyman!

Does hearing this jar your ears as much as it does mine? Don't get nervous: my point is not to mount a campaign against church marriages but to highlight one of the great benefits of studying the past. Much like traveling in a foreign country, when we figuratively "go" to the past we find that "they do things differently there," as one writer put it, and this helps us to become more self-conscious of how we do things in our own time and place.[9] In this instance, it was only when I learned that the Pilgrims condemned church marriage that I really became aware of my own opposing view. And by taking them seriously—instead of just saying to myself, "Boy, those Pilgrims were eccentric"—I was constrained to think more deeply about why I thought church marriage was important.

Here is what I concluded: whatever possible arguments might be made either for or against being married in the church, my dogmatic opinion on the matter was simply the one I had long ago absorbed by osmosis from my surroundings—in my case the Bible Belt of the 1970s in which I was raised. But the more important takeaway was the reminder that I, too, live in time,

---

[9]L. P. Hartley, *The Go-Between* (London: H. Hamilton, 1953), 1.

influenced substantially by the historical context in which I live and breathe and have my being.

This is the truth that historical consciousness weaves into our thinking. As it sinks in, it dawns on us that our *now* will be a future *then*. Generations to come will look back on us with a mixture of bewilderment and condescension. Hopefully, they will find much to admire. But they will also find much that is quaint, and ridiculous, and even repugnant, and they will assuredly marvel at our blindness to the power of the past over our lives.

As it matures, historical consciousness becomes more than a mindset. It becomes a mindset that engages the heart—mocking our pride, exposing our pretensions, and teaching us humility. In his book *Why Study History?*, author Rowan Williams, the former Archbishop of Canterbury, tells us that "there will always be gifts to be received from the past."[10] Humility may be the most priceless gift that history can bestow. As we saw in chapter three, the most common way to refute Henry Ford is to insist that the past is a storehouse of simple lessons (perhaps enlisting George Santayana to make our point). In this light,

> HUMILITY MAY BE THE MOST PRICELESS GIFT THAT HISTORY CAN BESTOW.

history turns into a body of knowledge to be mastered and applied *to the world around us*. In contrast, the humility born of historical consciousness opens us to the possibility of change

---

[10]Rowan Williams, *Why Study the Past?: The Quest for the Historical Church* (Grand Rapids: Eerdmans, 2005), 97.

within us, to the role that historical study can play in the trans-formative "inner work" of authentic education.

As rich as the rewards may be, there are other, potentially more compelling reasons to study history. In today's academic environment, educators almost always make a case for a particular course of study in terms of its *benefits*—individual and societal, material and "nonpecuniary." In the next chapter, we'll invert that argument and talk about *obligations*. For the Christian, the serious study of the past can be, above all, an expression of obedience and worship. Read on to understand why.

5

DISCIPLESHIP

■■■

BEFORE WRAPPING UP the first half of this little book, I want to approach the question "Why study the past?" from one other angle. I don't assume that everyone reading this book is a follower of Jesus, but I suspect that many of you are, and so I want to ask the following: Is there a specifically *Christian* case for the study of history? Should faith in the God of the Bible and the understandings of orthodox Christianity persuade us of the importance of the past?

I believe that it should, and I relish the opportunity to think out loud with you about why this might be true. This is a question I'm still working through, by the way, but this much I'm sure of: the Christian student is, by definition, called simultaneously to the love of God and the life of the mind, and figuring out how these twin callings are related is crucial to following either of them faithfully. This means that Christian historians need to take to heart our own variation of 1 Peter 3:15 and make ourselves "always . . . prepared to give an answer to everyone who asks" us why history is important. Here's my best defense:

First, *God created us to be historical beings*. If "human existence is historical existence," our belief in the Lord of creation convinces us that this is not by happenstance but by design. It is by *design* that we necessarily live in time. It is by *design* that "we live forward, but we can only think backward." It is by *design* that we cannot extricate ourselves from the power and presence of the past in our lives. It may not be this way in eternity—if Sheldon Vanauken is right, "timelessness" may be an attribute of heaven—but for now this is part of what it means to be human.[1] When we develop historical consciousness, we're actually training our minds to a greater self-awareness of how God has made us.

> Christianity is basically a vigorous appeal to history, a witness of faith to certain particular events in the past.
>
> Georges Florovsky

Second, *history is absolutely foundational to Christianity*. In one sense, this should not surprise us. Given how God has made us, how could it be otherwise? But it would be a huge mistake to pass lightly over history's indispensable role in the faith we profess. In the words of Georges Florovsky, a twentieth-century Russian Orthodox priest and historian, "Christianity is basically a vigorous appeal to history, a witness of faith to certain particular events in the past."[2]

---

[1]Sheldon Vanauken, *A Severe Mercy* (San Francisco: HarperSanFrancisco, 1977), 203-4.

[2]Georges Florovsky, "The Predicament of the Christian Historian," in *God, History, and Historians: Modern Christian Views of History*, ed. C. T. McIntire (New York: Oxford University Press, 1977), 407.

If you doubt him, look up the Apostles' Creed and note just how many of its assertions are historical claims. Christ "was conceived" by the Spirit, was "born" of the Virgin, "suffered" under Pilate, "was crucified, died, and was buried," "descended to hell," "rose again from the dead," "ascended to heaven." Do you see what the verbs have in common? The past tense is, quite literally, "essential to our language of faith."[3] This is not to minimize the importance of a living faith in the present—we all long to see the ongoing work of God in our lives—but to emphasize that the bedrock of the gospel is God's already completed work in Christ Jesus. As Stanley Hauerwas and William Willimon observe, our "faith begins, not in discovery, but in remembrance."[4]

Third, if we have accepted faith in Christ, *we are members of a community of faith that binds living and dead, present and past.* Not that we typically think of it that way. Occasionally a missionary on furlough will remind us that the church is truly transnational, and that the saints in eternity will encompass believers from "every tribe and language and people and nation" (Rev 5:9). But how many of us stop to think that the body of Christ transcends time as well as space? To paraphrase G. K. Chesterton, when we gather around the throne of God to proclaim "worthy is the Lamb," we'll join a chorus that "bridges the abyss of ages" as well as the "chasms of class," race, and ethnicity.[5]

---

[3]Margaret Bendroth, *The Spiritual Practice of Remembering* (Grand Rapids: Eerdmans, 2013), 6.

[4]Stanley Hauerwas and William H. Willimon, *Resident Aliens: Life in the Christian Colony* (Nashville: Abingdon, 1989), 52.

[5]G. K. Chesterton, *The Everlasting Man* (San Francisco: Ignatius Press, 1925), 32.

This is another way of calling attention to the Christian doctrine of "the communion of saints." That's a phrase in the Apostles' Creed we rarely pay much attention to, and I'm in no position to tell you exactly what it means. The hymn "The Church's One Foundation" sings of "mystic sweet communion with those whose race is won," and I agree with the hymn writer that there is an irreducible element of mystery in the concept. The nineteenth-century theologian Philip Schaff equated it to "the fellowship of all true believers living and departed."[6] Hauerwas and Willimon underscore the link between the doctrine and the importance of history: "The dead are not dead insofar as we are bound together in the communion of saints, living and dead," they write. "Therefore our conversation cannot be limited to those who now live."[7]

> The dead are not dead insofar as we are bound together in the communion of saints, living and dead. . . . Therefore our conversation cannot be limited to those who now live.
>
> Stanley Hauerwas and William Willimon

Fourth, *our faith informs us that the entire unfolding human story is worthy of attention*. It's not just the history of the church or of particular historical events that merit notice. We believe that God has infused the human story in general with great

---

[6]Philip Schaff, *The Creeds of Christendom, with a History and Critical Notes* (New York: Harper and Brothers, 1877), 1:22.
[7]Hauerwas and Willimon, *Resident Aliens*, 165.

dignity. To begin with, our understanding of creation tells us that God himself set the story in motion and that its central characters bear his image. Next, our belief in the incarnation reminds us that the Lord of the universe actually entered into the story, identifying with its characters and walking the earth as one of them.

Beyond this, our conviction of God's sovereignty teaches us that God is not only Creator but Sustainer as well. He is involved in the minutest details of human story. It is an epic that is unfolding according to his design and decree. In this sense we should see the human past as a sphere that God has created—and thus a form of natural revelation—every bit as much as the physical world around us. This makes studying history one expression of obedience to the divine command to love God with our minds—as well as with our heart, soul, and strength.

Fifth, *in striving to understand the past, we stand on holy ground.* Never forget the message of Lewis's "roaring cataract." The past is immense and incalculably complex, and most of it has fallen "off the world into total oblivion." As I noted in the opening chapter, when we contemplate this truth through eyes of faith, we should drop to our knees in awe and humility: awe as we reflect on the sheer magnitude of the never-ending past, and humility as we acknowledge our intellectual limitations. But above all, we should respond with worship as we marvel at the One who alone perfectly comprehends this vast expanse and declare with the psalmist, "Such knowledge is too wonderful for me" (Ps 139:6).

In the words of the late Arthur Link, "Biblical faith . . . tells us something very special about the historical record. It tells us that it is stored in its incredible totality in the mind and memory of God." In his essay "The Historian's Vocation," the former Princeton historian and one-time president of the American Historical Association expands on the implications of this realization.

It means that historical truth is God's truth, and thus precious to him. It means that when we claim to know any particle of the past truly, we are claiming to see it as God does, which should cause us to tremble. Finally, "while readily acknowledging that only God knows all historical truth," and that we necessarily understand it "only partially, imperfectly, corruptly," we can "affirm, profess, and confess" that when we strive to make sense of the past "we stand in the presence of something far greater than [ourselves]."[8]

> "Biblical faith . . . tells us something very special about the historical record. It tells us that it is stored in its incredible totality in the mind and memory of God."
>
> Arthur Link

Humanly speaking, the past is gone forever. We strive to reconstruct the merest fraction, relying on shadows and echoes to piece together glimpses of a vanished reality now stored in "the mind and memory of God." This is holy ground indeed. We need to take off our shoes.

---

[8]Arthur S. Link, "The Historian's Vocation," *Theology Today* 19 (1962/1963): 86, 82.

Finally, *historical understanding plays a vital role in faithful Christian discipleship.* We've already seen how history can function as a mirror, allowing us to see our own moment in time more clearly. In the light of Scripture, we see how precious such insight is and how risky historical ignorance can be. The letter to the Romans warns us about letting the world "squeeze [us] into its mould" (Rom 12:2, Phillips). The second letter to the Corinthians commands us to "take captive every thought to make it obedient to Christ" (2 Cor 10:5).

But when we're "stranded in the present," the fads of the moment can look like timeless truths. Because "we cannot imagine life any other way than it is," we can be shaped by our contemporary contexts without even realizing it. Nor can we "take captive every thought" when our present mindedness renders our most deeply ingrained ways of thinking invisible to us. In both cases, the first step to obeying the biblical commandment faithfully is seeing both ourselves and the world around us rightly. The study of history can further this goal.

History's ability to provide us with a memory before birth can be indispensable as well. One of the most repetitive observations of Scripture is the simple truth that our lives are short. We read that our days on earth are akin to a "breath," a "fleeting shadow," a "mist" (Job 7:7; Ps 144:4; Jas 4:14). And with brevity of life comes lack of perspective and narrowness of vision, which is precisely why we need to study the past.

"Remember the days of old," Moses sang to the assembly of Israel. "Consider the generations long past. / Ask your father and he will tell you, / your elders, and they will explain to you" (Deut 32:7). "Ask the former generation / and find out what their ancestors learned," counsels Bildad the Shuhite. And why is this necessary? Because "we were born only yesterday and know nothing" (Job 8:8-9). History allows us to glean wisdom from our ancestors, and in this respect, it is a logical extension of the biblical precept to honor age. It broadens our perspective and expands the range of experiences that we can draw on as we face the future.

> Remember the days of old;
>   consider the generations long past.
> Ask your father and he will tell you,
>   your elders, and they will explain to you.
>
> Deuteronomy 32:7

"Christianity is a religion of historians," wrote the French historian Marc Bloch from a Gestapo prison cell during World War II.[9] Surely he was right. Christians are, by vocation, called to be historians as well. God has created us as historical beings, implanted in us a historical faith, and bound us to the past by engrafting us into a historical church. When we approach the study of the past with humility and awe, recognizing the past as a sphere that God has ordained and prompted by biblical dictates and principles, the study of history can become both an act of obedience and an expression of worship. May it be so with us.

---

[9]Marc Bloch, *The Historian's Craft* (New York: Knopf, 1953), 4.

PART TWO

HOW TO STUDY HISTORY FAITHFULLY

6

LISTENING TO OTHER
HISTORIANS

■ ■ ■

NOW THAT YOU'RE INSPIRED to dive into the serious
study of history, let's talk about how to go about that. What does
it look like to study the past faithfully? We began part one with
a metaphor: the understanding of history as a form of memory,
an analogy that helps us to think through the crucial role that
engagement with the past plays in our lives. When it comes to
the question of faithful historical practice, I think it's useful to
begin with a different analogy, the understanding of history as a
form of *conversation*. It's a conversation that's been going on for
thousands of years, and one that will continue long after we're
"history" ourselves. The serious study of history begins when we
enter into it.

History is a conversation in two related but distinct senses. It
always involves a conversation in the present *about* the past; at
its best, it also involves, figuratively at least, a conversation in the
present *with* the past. I recommend that you keep these two
dimensions consciously in mind as you study. A lot of what I'll
be encouraging you to do in this part of the book is to practice

"metacognition," a fancy term that scholars use for self-consciously thinking about *how* we are thinking *as* we are thinking. As you cultivate such self-awareness, you'll discover that pretty much everything historians do falls under the heading of one or the other of these two forms of conversation. Because they have long since mastered these two kinds of dialogue, academic historians tend to switch back and forth between them without announcing the fact, but as you are starting out, it will help if you consciously name the type of conversation you are joining as you enter it.

This will be especially beneficial as you begin to think more intentionally about *evidence*. I like to compare evidence to the foundation of a house. In the long run, a house is no better than its foundation. It doesn't matter what kind of paint you slap on the siding or the color of the carpets in the family room; if the foundation is rotten, the structure is eventually going to come tumbling down. In the back of our minds, we know this. And yet we still focus on floor plans and color schemes and "curb appeal" as we search for our dream home. Who really wants to crawl under the house with a flashlight to check out the support beams?

> HISTORY ALWAYS INVOLVES A CONVERSATION IN THE PRESENT *ABOUT* THE PAST; AT ITS BEST, IT ALSO INVOLVES A CONVERSATION IN THE PRESENT *WITH* THE PAST.

In like manner, until we have been trained to do so, almost no one engrossed in an interesting historical narrative feels constrained to question the author's evidence before accepting the account as trustworthy. With the serious historian, however, this becomes second nature. Reflexively, we insist that the litmus test of responsible history is the quality of the evidence that undergirds it, and so we put on our coveralls, grab our flashlights, and spend a great deal of time under the house, thinking about the evidence that supports the stories we tell about the past. Simply put, when we pick up a work of history we tend to check out the footnotes or endnotes first, not last, on the grounds that a historical argument is never stronger than the evidence on which it is based.

Broadly speaking, all historical evidence can be classified into two main categories, which in turn correspond closely with the two kinds of conversation we can join. We enter into conversation *with* the past through the study of *primary sources*. Primary sources are forms of evidence that come directly from the period or persons or events

> SERIOUS HISTORIANS INSIST THAT THE LITMUS TEST OF RESPONSIBLE HISTORY IS THE QUALITY OF THE EVIDENCE THAT UNDERGIRDS IT.

we are seeking to understand. We enter into conversation *about* the past by engaging with *secondary sources*. Secondary sources are what historians produce when they look back on the past and try to make sense of it. They're also the gateway through which most of us enter the serious study of history. We'll focus on them for the rest of this chapter, and then turn to primary sources in chapter seven.

All serious study of the past begins in one of two contexts: outside of a classroom or inside of one. Over the years, I've met countless individuals who hated history as a subject in school but fell in love with it later in life. What prompted the transformation, more often than not, was their encounter with some kind of secondary source: a Hollywood movie "based on a true story," a visit to a "living history" site like Colonial Williamsburg or Plimoth Plantation, a Ken Burns documentary, a popular memoir, sometimes even a book by an academic historian. When asked, they explain that the movie or documentary or book made the past "come alive" and gave them an appetite for more. In essence, they had entered into a conversation in the present about the past, with the author or documentarian or docent or filmmaker relating to them what they themselves had learned.

For others of us, the serious study of history begins inside the classroom, and may, in fact, continue there for many years. Conversation *about* the past is the meat and potatoes of the history classroom, which is another way of saying that, even in advanced university courses, secondary sources are indispensable to the conversation that goes on there. In most history courses you can expect to engage with at least three

THERE ARE THREE SECONDARY SOURCES IN MOST HISTORY CLASSES: MONOGRAPHS, A SURVEY TEXTBOOK, AND AN INSTRUCTOR.

kinds of secondary sources. Sometimes there are one or more *monographs*. Frequently there is a *survey textbook*. Always, there is an *instructor*.

A *monograph* is a book-length secondary source that makes an argument about a comparatively narrow historical topic based on extensive research in primary sources. For instance, in my course on the American Revolution, I sometimes assign James Byrd's fine book, *Sacred Scripture, Sacred War*. Byrd was interested in one very particular question: When American colonists appealed to the Bible to support the cause of independence from Britain, exactly how did they do so? To answer the question, Byrd tracked down 543 pamphlets and published sermons that based political arguments on appeals to Scripture, and then he carefully analyzed the 17,148 biblical citations that they contained.[1]

In my course on the American Civil War, to cite another example, I often have students read Chandra Manning's monograph *What This Cruel War Was Over*. Manning, too, seeks to answer a narrow but hugely significant question: How did ordinary soldiers in the Civil War understand the relationship between the conflict and slavery? In her quest for an answer, she traveled to forty-five libraries, archives, and historical societies where she unearthed and analyzed the letters and diaries of well over a thousand Confederate and Union soldiers.[2]

Monographs are fairly common in advanced college courses, but introductory classes almost always feature a *survey textbook*—a thick, expensive, frequently less-than-scintillating overview of the subject of the course, typically something as vast in scope as the rise of Western civilization or the history of the world since 1500. Whereas monographs are narrowly focused

---

[1]James P. Byrd, *Sacred Scripture, Sacred War: The Bible and the American Revolution* (New York: Oxford University Press, 2013).

[2]Chandra Manning, *What This Cruel War Was Over: Soldiers, Slavery, and the Civil War* (New York: Alfred A. Knopf, 2007).

and deeply researched, the survey textbook is the opposite. Flying over at thirty thousand feet, survey texts offer a sweeping panorama of the landscape of the past without digging too deeply into any of the particulars.

It shouldn't surprise us to learn that the authors of survey texts rely predominantly on secondary sources in fashioning their narratives. How could it be otherwise? Think about it. Byrd and Manning each spent years in developing answers to questions that might merit a paragraph in a typical survey textbook. What historian—what team of historians—could craft a survey text based entirely on personal research in primary sources? By necessity, textbook authors construct their broad overviews by reading scores or hundreds of monographs, which they then synthesize into a larger account. This means that, no matter whose name is on the cover, survey texts are always the product of historical research by a large community of scholars.

This comes with benefits as well as costs. On the plus side, survey texts are great at conveying historical information. They're crammed with facts. They also strive, with somewhat less success, to promote historical understanding by suggesting ways to make sense of the thousands of discrete facts that they contain. They do this most commonly by calling attention to broad patterns and trends: the decline of feudalism, the rise of the nation-state, the spread of democracy, and so forth.

On the negative side, survey textbooks are rarely effective at modeling historical thinking skills. They may contain the occasional sidebar that reveals how historians have disagreed about a particular topic, but for the most part, they understate the complexity of the past as the price of covering a broad swath of the human experience. In the process, they tend to conceal the ways that trained historians actually think and the manner in which they sift through evidence to arrive at conclusions that are typically more tentative than the textbook lets on.

There is always one other secondary source in the history classroom—namely, the teacher or professor. This is easy to forget. He may look ancient, but your instructor didn't actually live through the Renaissance or the English Civil War, so when he's sharing his understanding of Machiavelli or Oliver Cromwell, that's exactly what he's doing, i.e., sharing *his* understanding. Don't get me wrong—your instructor may be quite knowledgeable about either or both, it's just that *he* is the one doing the talking, not Machiavelli or Cromwell.

In some courses, the instructor will be closely following an assigned textbook, which means that her elaborations and clarifications become essentially an extension of the text. In other instances, she will offer an interpretation that is very much her own, either arguing against the textbook or dispensing with a survey text entirely. In either case, the instructor is drawing on evidence about the past to help you make sense of it, which is the very definition of a secondary source.

So how do we go about engaging with secondary sources responsibly? I have five suggestions to make. They're less a formula to follow than a set of mental habits to practice until they become second nature. Each follows logically from the one that precedes it.

First, *cultivate epistemological humility*. That's a mouthful, but the meaning is simple. Epistemology is just the study of the nature of knowledge and how we acquire it, that is, how we know what we know. We cultivate epistemological humility by reminding ourselves of our limited ability to know the subject before us. It may seem counterintuitive, but sound historical thinking always starts here. Meditate on Lewis's "roaring cataract." Remind yourself—regularly, repeatedly—of the chasm that separates history and the past. Remember that the past is almost endless, human behavior is immeasurably complex, and the primary historical evidence that survives is but a miniscule fraction of the original historical record. Recognize the magnitude of the challenge. Feel small. Pray.

Second, *take the conversation metaphor seriously*. I don't care how dynamic the lecture is or how fascinating the book, you're not "going back in time" or watching "the past come alive." You're listening in on a conversation with other historians in the present about what the past may have been like and why it matters. And note that it's a highly *interpretive* conversation.

Professional historians are quick to distinguish between fact and interpretation. Facts can be objectively proved or disproved. The United States' formal entry into WWII began when Congress declared war against Japan on December 8, 1941, in direct response to the Japanese surprise attack against the American naval base at Pearl Harbor. This is unequivocally true. It is an objective fact that we can prove right down to the ground. But what course of events took the two nations to the brink of war, whether the conflict might have been avoided, and which policymakers or what global circumstances are most to blame for its onset are questions that the facts cannot nail down definitively. They lead to a thousand and one other questions and require the historian to piece together the available clues into a plausible scenario.

When it comes to answering big questions, historical facts never "speak for themselves." It's the historian who gives them a voice, breathing life into them by incorporating them into a larger interpretation. We often spend years in the archives digging for evidence, but this is just the first step in our quest for understanding. The heart of our work begins as we try to weave what we have uncovered into a coherent, persuasive interpretation. But here is the disturbing truth: for any question of considerable scope, there is always more than one logically plausible way to fit the surviving clues into a defensible explanation.

This doesn't mean that we have to accept all possible interpretations as equally valid. To say that there is more than one plausible way of interpreting the evidence is not to say that evidence no longer matters. When a crackpot contends that the Holocaust never happened, for example, we can point to the mountains of evidence to the contrary and dismiss the claim. Reliable historical evidence creates boundaries that we cannot cross without entering the realm of fiction. But within the area bounded by incontrovertible historical facts there will always be room for differences of opinion about how those facts fit together and what they mean. Interpretation involves an inescapable measure of subjectivity, even when undertaken with the utmost integrity. There will be disagreement.

Third, given how important interpretation is to the conversation, you should try to *get to know your conversation partner* before you read the book or listen to the lecture. Find out as much as you can about the authors of the secondary sources you are reading. As the prominent historian E. H. Carr put it more than a half century ago, "Study the historian before you begin to study the facts." Find out what "bees he has in his bonnet. When you read a work of history, always listen out for the buzzing."[3] I'm not sure that we get "bees in our bonnet" anymore, but his basic advice is sound. How we see the present influences how we see the past, and learning everything you can about the author's worldview can only help you in evaluating his interpretation. (But note: there's a fine line between making yourself aware of the author's possible bias and allowing your knowledge of the author to fuel biases of your own. The goal of getting to know the author is to enable you to engage with her more deeply, not to free you from thinking seriously about what she has to say.)

> Study the historian before you begin to study the facts.
>
> E. H. Carr

Fourth, always *focus on interpretation first and facts second*, not the other way around. For years we've all been told that the study of history is nothing more than the memorization of names and dates, with the result that we've been programmed to engage with secondary sources by looking for names and dates and other minutia while disregarding the

---

[3]Edward Hallett Carr, *What Is History?* (New York: Alfred A. Knopf, 1962), 25-26.

rest. I notice this sometimes in how my students take notes. I regularly shower them with brilliant reflections about the past that no one writes down but mention in passing that the Treaty of Guadalupe Hidalgo was negotiated by Nicholas P. Trist and ratified by the US Senate in 1848 and everyone is scribbling furiously.

Reverse the order of priority. Remember that the facts mean absolutely nothing when wrenched from the larger interpretation of which they are a part, so figure out what the interpretation is before getting bogged down with the facts. Perhaps you're thinking that it's impossible to discern the author's interpretation apart from the facts, but the reality is, you can. It's easiest with monographs. Academic historians almost always preface these narrowly focused studies with some kind of thesis statement—a

FOCUS ON INTERPRETATION FIRST AND FACTS SECOND.

debatable proposition about their topic that they intend to defend with evidence in the body of the book. In effect, they tell you the gist of their interpretation up front. But because these revelations tend to come in the introduction—and aren't infused with the sort of factual assertions we have been taught to look for—we tend to skip over these early pages in order to get to the "important" stuff.

With textbooks the task of figuring out the author's interpretation can be more challenging. Because the scope of such works is so broad, the interpretive stance of textbooks is typically harder to discern than for monographs, and it's much less common for them to argue a clear thesis from start to finish.

There are still clues to look for, however. Keep an eye out for anything that speaks to larger trends or patterns. What are the broad changes over time that the text is mapping? One of the best places to start is actually with the table of contents. If you're lucky, the chapter titles themselves can give you a rough sense of the overall arc of the survey. Within each chapter, read the introduction, the conclusion, and the titles of the intervening subsections. On the basis of this skeletal outline of the chapter, list what appear to be the most important generalizations that the author is making about the period or topic in question. Only then should you go back to read the chapter in its entirety.

Regardless of whether you're reading a monograph or a survey text, an awareness of the author's larger interpretation will allow you to read with a very specific question in mind: How do the authors defend the generalizations they are making? As you develop this habit, you'll be internalizing a way of thinking about history that sets apart the trained historian. The best history makes sense of the past through persuasive appeals to evidence.

One final piece of advice: *think long-term*. One of the reasons it's better to focus on interpretation is that you will eventually forget most of the facts anyway. The value of any course of historical study is best measured by how you and your understanding have been changed *after* you have forgotten most or all of the discrete facts. Stop regularly to take stock. What are the habits of mind you are acquiring? How are your historical understanding and consciousness being altered? Remember, the most powerful truth history can teach us is so ubiquitous that we often overlook it: the past was different from the present. The way things are now is the not the way they have always been, which should alert us to the likelihood that the way things are now is not how they will be. We, too, live in time.

7

LISTENING TO THE DEAD

■■■

NEXT, WE NEED TO THINK about how to work with primary sources. Recall that anything stemming directly from the time and place that interests us can serve as primary evidence. As a result, the range of possible primary sources is almost limitless.

Historians of the ancient past and of preliterate cultures rely heavily on surviving material artifacts: statuary, coins, household wares, monument inscriptions, and architectural ruins, to name some of the most common. Historians of more recent eras can also gain insight from such visual and material sources—historians at Mount Vernon have even excavated garbage pits in search of clues about the diet of George Washington's slaves—but they have traditionally relied predominantly on written or printed documents. These include popular and elite literature, diaries, letters, newspapers, pamphlets, maps, city directories, broadsides, song lyrics, advertisements, wills, deeds, tax records, trial transcripts, and legislative journals, among others. Students of the more recent past can also glean insight from oral testimony, as well as from a range of electronic and digital media, including radio broadcasts, television programs, and movies. Future historians of this generation will study us in part through our YouTube videos, blog posts, Instagram photos, and tweets.

Primary sources lie at the foundation of all serious historical research and argument. Remember that they constitute the medium for a different type of conversation than the one we have with secondary sources: a conversation *with* the past instead of *about* the past. But as a double benefit, as you gain experience in working with primary sources, you'll also find that you're better equipped to evaluate secondary sources intelligently. Having personally grappled with the challenges of teasing insight from these shadows of the past, you'll find it easier to think along with the authors of secondary works as they fashion interpretations from similar kinds of evidence.

So how do we engage with primary sources responsibly? Rather than give you a laundry list of steps to follow, I'd rather underscore the qualities of heart and mind that are essential. I emphasize three: love, discernment, and—again—humility.

To understand the value of each to the historian, we need to go back and take seriously the metaphor of conversation

> PRIMARY SOURCES CONSTITUTE THE MEDIUM FOR A CONVERSATION *WITH* THE PAST INSTEAD OF *ABOUT* THE PAST.

with the past. Whenever we engage with primary sources, there's always a strong temptation to think of the document or artifact before us as nothing more than a source of information. It carries the potential to help us get what we want, whether it's an A on the assignment or the acclaim of professional peers.

The study of history is transformed when we abandon that utilitarian mindset and begin to think of the primary sources as echoes or shadows of living beings. The stakes get so much higher—and the rewards incomparably greater—as we admonish ourselves to remember the flesh and blood on the other side of the evidence. As the historian Georges Florovsky observed, "The ultimate purpose of a historical inquiry is not in the establishment of certain objective facts," as absolutely indispensable as that is, "*but in the encounter with living beings.*"[1] Whether the sources hint of individuals or groups, the famous or the forgotten, what we're really about is listening for the whispers of those who have gone before us.

Or as historian Beth Schweiger puts it in language calculated to grab our attention, the goal of the historian is "to make a relationship with the dead." Our conversation partners are real human beings, creatures of inestimable value, made for eternity by the Father whose image they bear. When we take this to heart, it changes everything. Our goal can't be to *use* these unsuspecting individuals for our own purposes. We have to *love* them. This is Schweiger's conclusion as well. "In history," she writes, "the call to love one's neighbor is extended to the dead."[2]

---

[1]Georges Florovsky, "The Predicament of the Christian Historian," in *God, History, and Historians: Modern Christian Views of History,* ed. C. T. McIntire (New York: Oxford University Press, 1977), 418, italics added.
[2]Beth Barton Schweiger, "Seeing Things: Knowledge and Love in History," in *Confessing History: Explorations in Christian Faith and the Historian's Vocation,* ed. John Fea, Jay Green, and Eric Miller (Notre Dame: University of Notre Dame Press, 2010), 61.

> In history, the call to love one's neighbor is extended to the dead.
>
> Beth Schweiger

So it all begins with *love*—not Hallmark Channel infatuation but a mature act of the will, the purposeful determination to seek our neighbor's good. That sounds noble, but what does it actually look like in action? In many respects, it resembles how we show love to the living. It begins simply by *noticing*, by consciously acknowledging the living beings who once animated the artifacts before us. This is why, whenever feasible, I like to have students read written primary sources in the original handwriting of their authors, rather than in the bloodless transcriptions of primary source anthologies.

Beyond noticing, loving the dead will necessarily involve *listening carefully* to what they have to say and *respecting their perspective*. The latter doesn't require us to agree with them, but it does call us to the hard work of trying to understand their point of view and being *open to learning from them*. And make no mistake, if their point of view contradicts our own, this will require love. In the middle of the last century, the British historian Herbert Butterfield concluded that "the whole range of history is a boundless field for the constant exercise of Christian charity," precisely because of the recurring need to "catch the outlook and feelings of men not like-minded with oneself."[3]

---

[3]Herbert Butterfield, *History and Human Relations* (New York: Macmillan, 1952), 146.

At bottom, loving the dead as a historian is a lot like practicing hospitality to the living. Think of yourself as a host or hostess. Figuratively, you're inviting a stranger into your home for coffee and conversation, and you're doing your best to treat your guest as you would want to be treated if the roles were reversed. It's a profoundly personal act and, by God's grace, a genuinely loving one.

But love without *discernment* can lead us astray. It may sound contradictory at first, but we have to combine our love for our historical neighbors with a measure of skepticism or suspicion, a conscious resolve not to take what they tell us automatically at face value. (Yes, there's an irresolvable tension here; good historical practice is not for the faint-hearted.) One part of our job as historians is to love the dead, but another crucial part is to determine the trustworthiness of the evidence they left us. We can love figures from the past without swallowing everything that they tell us. We can question what they tell us while still treating them with respect.

This is quite countercultural, by the way. On the whole, contemporary Americans aren't very good at constructive disagreement. This is in large part because we get so little practice at it. Our technology allows us to withdraw into miniature communities of the like-minded, with the result that our critical thinking skills atrophy and we lose the ability either to persuade or to learn from those who see the world differently.

In contrast, sound historical thinking absolutely requires that we think critically (i.e., analytically) about our conversation partners even as we strive to learn from them. In this respect, we function less like a host or hostess showing hospitality to a guest than as a juror trying to determine the credibility of a witness. The goal is to get to the point where, when presented with a primary source, you automatically weigh its strengths and weaknesses in order to arrive at an accurate sense of its value. What questions can the source address? How reliable are the answers it offers?

There are any number of ways to go about this, but the process always involves putting the primary source in a larger historical context. (Remember—no context, no meaning.) You'll often need to know the larger context simply to *understand* what the source is telling you. Written documents, for example, will regularly allude to places or persons or events that the author felt no need to explain but which will be mysterious to us without further digging. But you'll also need to study the context of the source as you determine whether to *believe* what it is telling you. Here your preeminent task is to determine the credibility of the source. The advice that I offer below alludes to written or printed documents, since that is the most common kind of primary evidence that historians start out with, but the underlying principles apply generally to the range of primary sources that historians can consult.

Remember E. H. Carr's advice to "study the historian" before you dive into a secondary textbook or monograph? The same principle applies when we engage with primary sources. Before examining the message, you need to find out everything you can about the messenger. Start with the author's *identity*: What do you know about him or her? Do you have any clues concerning the author's personal character, potential biases, or abilities of judgment? Be sure to delve into *motive*: Why was the document created to begin with? Was it written intentionally to be published or expected to be kept private? Did the author have an incentive to be accurate, or perhaps a motive to misrepresent? Who was the intended *audience*, and how might this affect the author's candor or emphasis?

Don't forget to ask yourself what *authority* the author brings to the conversation: Is the writer describing her current state of mind or events which she just witnessed directly? Is he an old man recalling occurrences from his youth or relating second-hand accounts of distant happenings? Finally, keep track of the testimony of other witnesses, what we might call *external corroboration*. Do other primary sources contradict or affirm what the author of the source at hand would have you believe? Remember that the goal of these questions is to help you in practicing discernment. Jurors who assume that all witnesses are reliable are abdicating their responsibility.

Although love and discernment are both essential as we strive to "make a relationship with the dead," in the end they're not enough. We also need a liberal dose of *humility*. As we discussed in chapter six, when we're reading secondary sources, we must remind ourselves that historians' ability to reconstruct the past is always limited by a lack of evidence, among other things. We simply don't have enough to go on to arrive at definitive answers to the questions that interest us. When it comes to engaging with primary sources, we have to humble ourselves even further. The truth is, even when we're staring the relevant evidence full in the face, our natural tendency will be to misunderstand it. In sum, only part of the challenge we face lies with the evidence. Part of it lies in *us*.

No one has explained this point better than Stanford educational psychologist Sam Wineburg. For more than three decades,

Wineburg has been meticulously studying the ways that trained historians think as they engage with historical evidence and comparing that to the way that history has been most commonly taught in the classroom. The gist of his findings is captured by the title of his seminal work, *Historical Thinking and Other Unnatural Acts*. Sound historical thinking doesn't come naturally. Why is this?

> SOUND HISTORICAL THINKING DOESN'T COME NATURALLY.

The answer lies in how our brains respond when we come across something new. Whenever we study the past, we always encounter some combination of the familiar and the strange. The people that we figuratively meet in the past will be like us in some ways, for example, and very different from us in others. The familiar aspects we can process easily and accurately, but the elements of the past that are truly foreign can cause problems. This is because our brains are wired to learn by analogy. When we encounter something that we have never seen before, we rummage through the file cabinets of our minds in search of something that looks similar. We then use the closest match that we can find and use it to label the new thing that we have found.

As Wineburg points out, this is all perfectly natural and reasonable. It can also be grossly misleading. He makes the point with a memorable anecdote from the travels of Marco Polo. When the thirteenth-century Venetian explorer was exploring the interior of Sumatra, he came upon a remarkable animal that probably no other European had ever laid eyes on. As he recorded in his journal, the dark, enormous beast featured a "single large, black horn in the middle of the forehead." Having

never seen or even heard of a rhinoceros, Polo reluctantly concluded that he had met his first unicorn. Admittedly, the ugly
brute looked nothing like the animals "as we describe them
when . . . they let themselves be captured by virgins."[4] But what
else could it be?

Here is Wineburg's troubling conclusion: each of us naturally follows the exact same cognitive process that Marco Polo
was unconsciously employing when he mislabeled those Su-
matran rhinos. And because when we delve into primary
sources we will regularly en-counter ways of thinking and
being that are strange to us, we will perpetually be in
danger of making the same kind of mistake. Academic

> **PRESENTISM IS OUR UNTHINKING INCLINATION TO VIEW THE PAST THROUGH THE LENS OF THE PRESENT AND TO MISREAD WHAT WE ARE SEEING AS A RESULT.**

historians refer to this as the problem of *presentism*—our un-
thinking inclination to view the past through the lens of the
present and to misread what we are seeing as a result.

The good news is that we can train our minds to combat this
present mindedness. The first step, as Lucy says to Charlie
Brown, is to admit that we have a problem. Presentism isn't
"some bad habit we've fallen into."[5] It's how all of us instinctively
make sense of the past, and it regularly gets us in trouble.

---

[4]Sam Wineburg, *Historical Thinking and Other Unnatural Acts: Charting the Future of Teaching the Past* (Philadelphia: Temple University Press, 2001), 24.

[5]Wineburg, *Historical Thinking*, 19.

Unicorns are lurking everywhere. The way forward, paradoxically, is by disciplining our minds to doubt our natural ability to understand the past. By learning to be suspicious of our first impressions, we can actually mitigate the distortion of presentism and hear the dead more accurately than we might otherwise.

The most effective historical thinkers, Wineburg explains, don't make snap judgments when wrestling with primary sources. What sets them apart is actually their expertise at "cultivating puzzlement." Of course they form first impressions along the way—it is impossible not to—but they have learned through practice to "stand back" from them, to hold their initial impressions lightly as they continue to listen and think and probe and evaluate.[6]

Wineburg illustrates his point by describing a field experiment in which he asked a series of college students each individually to make sense of a collection of primary documents from Abraham Lincoln and explain to him how they did so. On the surface, the sources seemed to suggest that Lincoln was inconsistent, opposing slavery as immoral while tolerating inequality. As Wineburg relates, some students immediately concluded that Lincoln had contradicted himself and moved on. Others sought to explain the contradiction, but they did so by applying their presentist understandings of the contemporary world. Lincoln was just like our current-day "spin doctors," they concluded. He wanted above all to get elected, and so he cynically altered his message to suit his

---

[6]Wineburg, *Historical Thinking*, 21-22.

audience. There was a certain plausibility to this interpretation, but as Wineburg notes, what these students had actually done was to resolve Lincoln's apparent contradictions by turning him "into one of us," by making him "our contemporary in a top hat."[7]

Wineburg then broadened his study by inviting several history professors to make sense of the same documents. One of the professors that he characterizes at length was a historian named Bob Alston who knew very little about Lincoln beforehand but who eventually arrived at a sophisticated reading of the documents. What most distinguished Alston's approach from the undergraduates' was not the relevant factual knowledge he brought to the sources—that was minimal—but his willingness to postpone judgment while wrestling with the apparent contradiction in Lincoln's views.

Alston's reading of the documents was an extended exercise in the "specification of ignorance." He identified passages that didn't immediately make sense and made a mental list of questions that he couldn't answer. Above all, he insisted on the possibility that the contradictions he perceived were apparent only, that they only seemed inconsistent because he didn't yet understand Lincoln's world. This simple act of self-doubt became a fruitful starting point for deeper inquiry. How would Lincoln have to see the world to arrive logically at conclusions that now strike us as inconsistent? The answer wasn't immediately apparent, but in the end, Alston's self-doubt was a springboard to fuller understanding. As Wineburg concludes, "Other readers

---

[7]Wineburg, *Historical Thinking*, 18-19.

used these documents to confirm their prior beliefs. They encountered the past here and labeled it. Alston encountered the past and learned from it."[8]

So can you.

---

[8]Wineburg, *Historical Thinking*, 20, 22.

8

CONTRIBUTING TO
THE CONVERSATION

■■■

SO FAR OUR DISCUSSION OF HISTORY as a form of
conversation has been focused on listening—listening to other
historians, listening to the dead. But sooner or later you may
want to contribute to the conversation yourself (or you may be
required to do so). Most history primers include chapters on
how to write a good history paper, and my guess is that none of
them will ever become the basis of a major motion picture. That
is to say, while the study of the human past can be endlessly
fascinating and even life changing, discussions of historical research methods are rarely scintillating, and typically the more
practical and specific they are, the more boring they become.

If you're a new historian on the verge of starting your own
research project, you'd probably benefit from advice on how to
locate evidence, take notes, prepare drafts, and cite sources,
among other topics. I'm going to leave those practical tips to
your instructor (if you're doing research in the context of an
academic course) or to any one of the numerous books on historical research methods readily available through libraries and

bookstores. In the few pages available here, I'd rather focus on habits of mind that will enhance not only the quality of your research but its personal benefits as well.

But first a word of warning: history papers are hard work. They can be incredibly rewarding, but they're also the most demanding thing a new historian has to do, and our natural tendency will be to make them even harder by procrastinating. A good rule of thumb is to allow at least twice as much time for each step of the process as you think it should take. Historical research is messy, and successful research projects often involve multiple false starts before you begin to gain momentum. In fact, I'd argue that the single hardest part of an effective history paper comes at the very beginning as you work to nail down an appropriate topic.

Coming up with a workable topic is a process of converting a general subject that interests you into a specific question that you have both the time and the resources to answer. Beware of biting off more than you can chew. The temptation is to pose questions that are too broad to answer effectively given the evidence available and the time you have to analyze it. If you have a few weeks to produce a required eight- to ten-page paper for your US history survey course, for example, a paper on the causes of the Civil War or the long-term effects of European immigration is far too ambitious. As we have seen, academic historians maintain that history is reliable only to the degree that it is grounded persuasively in trustworthy evidence, and topics that expansive would require years (decades?) to research adequately.

HISTORICAL RESEARCH IS MESSY.

There is no hard and fast standard for determining if a particular topic is too broad. The answer will vary depending on the time and resources at your disposal, but this much I can guarantee: coming up with an effective paper topic is an iterative process in which you repeatedly narrow and refine and clarify your original idea, and that takes time. Allow for it.

For the sake of discussion, let's imagine that you've already identified a good question to explore and are ready to proceed. What next? How can you maximize the educational benefits of the hard work that lies ahead? The short answer is twofold. First, practice metacognition—be as self-conscious as you can in thinking about how you are thinking as you proceed. Second, work to shape your thinking to conform more and more with the best historical practice. The end goal is to internalize the right habits of mind until they become second nature. To use the categories I introduced in chapter three, the goal is not only to increase what you know but also to alter how you think. The process of writing a history paper can help promote that kind of transformation.

Before jumping into the fine details, let's start with the big picture. You're about to begin a research project. What does that really mean? Here the metaphors for history that we've developed so far will be useful. One of the striking features of a history paper is that it combines both of the kinds of *conversation* that we considered in chapters six and seven. An effective history paper listens to the dead in order to speak to the living. It begins in conversation *with* the past as you conduct intensive research in primary sources. It then morphs into conversation *about* the past as you communicate what you think you have learned.

If you are conducting your research for an academic course, your instructor may even require you to include a *historiographical* section in your paper. *Historiography* is a

> **AN EFFECTIVE HISTORY PAPER LISTENS TO THE DEAD IN ORDER TO SPEAK TO THE LIVING.**

fancy word for the study of the study of history, especially with regard to how academic interpretations of the past have changed over time. By discussing the historiography of your subject, you'll be explicitly situating your research within the larger ongoing conversation among historians relative to your topic. Whether or not you include such a feature, you should definitely think of your paper as addressing a contemporary audience. If your research is worth pursuing, it should result in something important to share with the living.

This is because your goal is not simply to speak to the living, but to be a blessing to them. Here the metaphor of history as a *mirror* is instructive. It reminds us that we study the past on its own terms but not for its own sake. Our starting point as historians is the conviction that knowledge of the past is essential to seeing and understanding the present. Academic historians label those who study the past wholly as an end in itself *antiquarians*, and they don't mean it as a compliment. The antiquarian is solely preoccupied with "old stuff," the French scholar Marc Bloch explained in *The Historian's Craft*. "The master quality of the historian," in contrast, is the "faculty of understanding the living."[1] What could be more precious?

---

[1] Marc Bloch, *The Historian's Craft* (New York: Knopf, 1953), 43.

Note that Bloch's conception of the historian's "master quality" dovetails nicely with the traditional Christian understanding of vocation. For at least five centuries, the preponderance of Protestant thought on vocation has linked the concept of calling to the service of the "common good" or "the need others have of us."[2] If your subject has nothing to say to your audience that is relevant to the here and now, you haven't found the right topic yet.

But as you're researching the past in order to serve the present, never forget that the facts you're uncovering won't speak for themselves. When his students applauded his lecture on the superiority of French institutions, the nineteenth-century French historian Fustel de Coulanges is supposed to have cut short their ovation. "Gentlemen, do not applaud," he objected modestly. "It is not I who speak, but history that speaks through me."[3] It was a noble and grand declaration and also a bunch of hooey. History is not an academic séance in which we channel the dead, nor is it a kind of intellectual safari in which we brave the dangers of the archives and bring back "the past" like a trophy to mount on the wall.

Here the metaphor of history as *memory* is key, for it reminds us, above all, of the foundational truth that history isn't the past itself. A persuasive interpretation of the past isn't just sitting there in the archives, obscured by cobwebs and waiting to be discovered. Rather, it's something that we actively construct as

---

[2]William C. Placher, ed., *Callings: Twenty Centuries of Christian Wisdom on Vocation* (Grand Rapids: Eerdmans, 2005), 262, 423.

[3]Carl L. Becker, "What Are Historical Facts?," *Western Political Quarterly* 8 (1955): 334.

we piece together surviving clues with the help of logical analysis and informed imagination. This means that writing an effective history paper is an exercise in creating as much as discovering.

In sum, if you're about to write a history paper, you're about to produce something new, something that is more than the sum of the individual facts that go into it. It will be new because of the *interpretation* of the evidence that you contribute. My sense is that students often find that word intimidating, by the way. *Interpretation* seems to connote brilliant insights and wholly original understandings, and pretty soon you're thinking, "Who am I to come up with an interpretation?" (The only word that is scarier is *analysis*.)

It will take some of the pressure off, perhaps, to speak instead in terms of *judgment*. With apologies to Fustel de Coulanges, it is impossible to write an effective history paper without exercising judgment. It's your job to judge what the facts mean and how they fit together. This is why academic historians often think of an interpretation as making an *argument*. Your goal is to *prove* something, to offer a persuasive answer to a question based on your judgment of the evidence. If you're successful, when you're done you will have added to your reader's understanding of the past.

Doing so will require that you draw on the habits of mind we have already discussed in chapters six and seven. Because historical evidence forms the bedrock of an effective history paper, the principles we've considered for analyzing primary and secondary sources will all be relevant. But producing a persuasive interpretation requires more. Interpretation is about making connections; it involves weaving together evidence into a larger

INTERPRETATION IS ABOUT MAKING CONNECTIONS; IT INVOLVES WEAVING TOGETHER EVIDENCE INTO A LARGER STORY ABOUT THE PAST THAT EXPLAINS AND EDIFIES.

story about the past that explains and edifies.

So what are the habits of mind that trained historians employ as they exercise judgment to fashion interpretations? A few years back, professors Thomas Andrews and Flannery Burke set out to identify precisely the habits of mind that "stand at the heart of the questions historians seek to answer, the arguments we make, and the debates in which we engage." Andrews and Burke labeled the habits they pinpointed the "five C's of historical thinking."[4] Their list is not sacrosanct—other scholars might come up with a different list or use different terminology—but it has caught on among educators as a convenient rubric for the classroom. The five habits that Andrews and Burke identified are change over time, context, causality, contingency, and complexity. An effective research paper will reflect each of these, either implicitly or explicitly. Let's take each in turn.

Attention to *change over time* is so central to historical thinking that we can actually overlook it, missing the forest for the trees. Trained historians conceive of the world as *unfolding*. We think of the present as inextricably intertwined with the past, and we make sense of pretty much everything by situating it in the larger flow of human experience across time. Time isn't just a variable

---

[4]Thomas Andrews and Flannery Burke, "What Does It Mean to Think Historically?," *Perspectives* 45, no. 1 (January 2007): 32-35.

that we bring to the study of the world. It's "the very lens through which [we] see."[5]

Want to know how to frame good historical questions? Ask about change over time. Academic historians do this consistently in the ques-

> AN EFFECTIVE RESEARCH PAPER WILL REFLECT CHANGE OVER TIME, CONTEXT, CAUSALITY, CONTINGENCY, AND COMPLEXITY.

tions that drive their books. What were the roots of the Protestant Reformation? the causes of the Russian Revolution? the social consequences of Reconstruction? the economic implications of the New Deal? Do you see how change over time is intrinsic to each of these questions? But note that you can't answer any of them effectively without also addressing *context* as well as *causality* (the relation of cause and effect). This is because academic historians are trained not only to describe but to explain. It's not enough to determine what happened in the past. We also want to know why things unfolded as they did.

We've already discussed how important it is to consider the context of individual primary documents if we hope to understand them correctly. Trained historians bring that same sensitivity to context to their broader interpretations of the past. It's not just individual documents that emerge from a historical setting—so does every person, group, event, or trend that can possibly figure in the pages of our essays and books. They "all

---

[5]C. S. Lewis, *The Great Divorce* (New York: Macmillan, 1946), 122. The actual quote, which Lewis puts imaginatively in the mouth of the nineteenth-century writer George MacDonald, is "Time is the very lens through which ye see."

develop within a tightly interwoven world," as Andrews and Burke observe.[6] That makes attention to context imperative.

In like manner, our determination to explain the patterns that we observe leads us inevitably to the contemplation of cause and effect. This is why E. H. Carr could conclude that "the study of history is a study of causes."[7] But note that historians cannot nail down cause and effect in the same way that scientists do. Scientists can devise a theory about how two compounds interact and then test it repeatedly under controlled conditions in the laboratory until they are confident that they know what's going on. Historians get to make only one indirect observation, always on the basis of incomplete and imperfect evidence, from which they formulate a tentative conjecture about cause and effect. History is unavoidably a study of causes, but establishing causation is the most difficult thing a historian can undertake.

Proving cause and effect is made all the harder because we take *contingency* so seriously. To say that the past is contingent is to insist that no historical outcome is inevitable. Any given occurrence in the past was dependent on a number of prior factors, each of which in turn depended on some number of other factors, and so on, ad infinitum. Change any one of these countless variables, and the final outcome may have been altered dramatically. At bottom, the concept of contingency reminds us of the unpredictability of human behavior and the intense interrelatedness of human experience in our "tightly interwoven world."

---

[6] Andrews and Burke, "What Does It Mean to Think Historically?," 33.
[7] Edward Hallett Carr, *What Is History?* (New York: Alfred A. Knopf, 1962), 113.

Academic historians stress contingency not only because it informs how we understand what happened in the past, but also because it helps us to appreciate how people in the past experienced their present. Each of us goes through life not knowing what the next day will bring, yet as historians we regularly know the future of the figures we study. Not only does this tempt us to feel superior—since we know more than our subjects did—but it also makes it difficult to put ourselves in their place as we seek to understand them. It was this sense of knowing "too much" that once prompted the British historian Catherine Wedgewood to cry out, "In vain have I longed to recapture that blessed ignorance."[8] I'm not sure all experienced historians would go that far, but we do recognize that hindsight can be a liability as well as an asset. Emphasizing contingency is one way of trying to limit its negative effects.

The fifth "C" of historical thinking, *complexity*, follows naturally from its four companions. Far from the mindless memorization of names and dates, our goal is to comprehend a messy world. We not only acknowledge its complexity, we relish it. The interrelatedness of human experience and the unpredictability of human behavior convince us that simple explanations are typically bad explanations. We're reflexively skeptical of them. We know that the complexity of any given aspect of the past only increases the more that we learn of it. Conversely, the patterns of the past are clearest for those periods we know little about. "To the naked eye there is a face in

---

[8] C. V. Wedgewood, *Truth and Opinion: Historical Essays* (London: Collins, 1960), 37.

the moon," C. S. Lewis observed, but "it vanishes when you use a telescope."[9]

So there, briefly, are the "five C's of historical thinking," and here I could stop, but I want to close with a word of exhortation. *Be excited about what lies ahead.* I began this chapter by stressing that historical research is hard work. To maximize its benefits, I've challenged you to practice metacognition, which can be mentally exhausting in its own right. But don't lose sight of the big picture. If you're about to embark on your own original research project, you're on the cusp of an amazing opportunity. Remember that history is not the past itself, but the remembered past. Quite literally, you're being invited to "make history."

Now go and do it.

9

WHY DOES IT MATTER?

■■■

BOILED DOWN, most of what trained historians do in their investigations is describe and explain. We ask what happened in the past and why. But we also need to *evaluate*, to meditate on the meaning of what we are learning. In sum, at some point we have to stop and wrestle with the significance *to the present* of the knowledge we're acquiring. We have to ask ourselves, "So what? Why does this matter, *now*, to me?"

Academic historians typically aren't very comfortable with the "so what?" question. We're convinced that the careful study of the past can cast valuable light on the present, yet in our formal academic writing we rarely reflect openly on how our research might serve the common good, nor do we discuss how we ourselves live in the light of what we have learned. Indeed, when we do refer to the significance of our specialized research, we usually have in mind the "historiographical contribution" we are making, by which we mean the way that our research complements or contradicts the arguments advanced by other scholars.

As a Christian, I find the academic attention to historiographical significance not wrong, in and of itself, but badly incomplete. If the historical conversation is, in part, a discussion in the present about the past, then historians who are trying to contribute to that conversation understandably need to know what other historians have argued about the topic. But if the human past is a sphere that God has created and superintends—and in this sense a form of natural revelation—then we ought to expect much more from our historical study than historiographical accomplishment alone. If the figures from the past that we study were created in God's image, just like we are, if they were limited by their fallenness and finitude, just like we are, then surely there are truths in their stories that can speak to ours as well. There are many ways to think about gleaning a larger meaning from our historical study, but in this concluding chapter I want to explore what it might mean to make the study of the past a part of a larger quest for a heart of wisdom. I cannot give you a precise formula to follow, but here are some suggestions that may be helpful.

To begin with, train your mind to *expect life-changing insight*, and be proactive in seeking it. Here are three open-ended questions that you should ask periodically in the course of your historical studies:

"How does what I am learning inform how I see the world?"

"How does it change how I understand myself?"

"What does the knowledge that I am acquiring require of me?"

In mentioning this final question, my mind goes to Steven Garber's wonderful book *Visions of Vocation*. In it, the author repeatedly asks one simple question: What will you do with what you know? Garber doesn't mean what kind of job are you going to get after graduation. Instead, he's challenging us to think about how to use the knowledge we've acquired to love our neighbors and serve the common good. Although we often live as if we think otherwise, knowledge always comes with moral responsibility.[1]

Next, keep in mind that *the proper focus of historical research is human beings, not God.* If you're a Christian, this principle may surprise and even trouble you. Over the years, countless well-meaning Christians have wanted to add a fourth question to the three listed above—namely, "What am I learning about how God has been at work in the past?" A prominent example of this line of inquiry would be the most widely read Christian interpretation of US history ever published, *The Light and the Glory*, by Pastor Peter Marshall and David Manuel. The authors described their study as "a search for the hand of God in the different periods of our nation's beginnings."[2]

> KNOWLEDGE ALWAYS COMES WITH MORAL RESPONSIBILITY.

Scholars label such efforts to trace God's handiwork in the past *providential history.* As a Christian, there are elements of this approach that I very much respect. It challenges the unrelenting naturalism that today's secular academy demands, the insistence that all historical occurrences be explained with reference to "strictly natural laws and forces, with strictly natural origins and

---

[1]Steven Garber, *Visions of Vocation: Common Grace for the Common Good* (Downers Grove, IL: InterVarsity Press, 2014).

[2]Peter Marshall and David Manuel, *The Light and the Glory* (Old Tappan, NJ: Fleming H. Revell, 1977), 22.

consequences."[3] It takes God's sovereignty in human affairs with admirable seriousness, and it wrestles with a question—"Where is God in history?"—that every Christian should recognize as vital.

You should know, however, that almost all academic historians—including scholars of faith—reject providential history as inappropriate, if not illegitimate. They conceive of the academy as a pluralistic public space and believe as a matter of principle that the conversation that takes place there should be open to all. With regard to history, this means that Christian scholars are welcome to participate, but they must be willing to play by "the rules of the academic game," as one prominent Christian historian phrased it.[4] They do this by basing their arguments on forms of evidence that all parties at the table can potentially find persuasive. Appeals to divine intervention don't meet this requirement.

But in addition to academic conventions, there are even more compelling *theological* reasons to forego providential interpretation. To begin with, to the degree that we take it seriously, the doctrine of God's exhaustive sovereignty means that providence simply isn't a helpful explanatory variable. Remember, Paul taught the church at Ephesus that God "works out *everything* in conformity with the purpose of his will" (Eph 1:11, italics added). In light of this teaching, as Christian historian Jonathan Boyd observes, "It makes little sense to name some events as more

---

[3]Jonathan Tucker Boyd, "This Holy Hieroglyph: Providence and Historical Consciousness in George Bancroft's Historiography" (PhD diss., Johns Hopkins University, 1999), 242.

[4]George M. Marsden, *The Outrageous Idea of Christian Scholarship* (New York: Oxford University Press, 1997), 44.

providential than others."[5] Yet if we were to apply the doctrine systematically, it would effectively oblige us to explain every event in world history with the same three little words: *God willed it*. This is why Christian academics commonly conceive of historical explanation as the identification of *secondary* causes, that is, of the means that the Lord employs in effecting his will.

In reality, practitioners of providential history rarely apply the doctrine of divine sovereignty systematically, nor are they content to rest with the assertion that God works in human history. Discerning God's *purpose* is their higher goal. *The Light and the Glory*, for example, informed readers that "God had a definite and extremely demanding plan for America" and, what is more, that the authors had discovered what it was.[6] In sum, providential history typically purports to prove not simply that God *is* at work but also *why*—that is, how a particular historical occurrence fits within God's overarching design.

Such a question should be of great interest to any Christian, but when we expect to answer it by means of ordinary historical research, we are expecting more from our study of the past than God promises. Granted, the historical books of the Old Testament regularly explain how God was at work in the lives of kings and nations, but we must never forget that those books are part of God's special revelation. Their authors were divinely inspired, their words literally "God-breathed" (2 Tim 3:16). The interpretations of the past that historians produce today are in an entirely different category.

[5]Jonathan Tucker Boyd, "If We Ever Needed the Lord Before," *Books and Culture*, May/June 1999, 40.
[6]Marshall and Manuel, *Light and the Glory*, 22.

So does this require us to set aside the question "Where is God in history?" and pretend it's not important? Not at all, but when we come across dogmatic assertions concerning "God's plan for America" or the Lord's purpose behind this or that historical occurrence not discussed in Scripture, we need to realize that no one can arrive at such conclusions on the basis of ordinary analysis of historical evidence. In fact, they're not historical conclusions at all. They are prophetic declarations, and that's what we need to call them.

Even when we set aside appeals to providence, however, the study of history still affords a marvelous framework for life-changing moral inquiry, provided that we emphasize moral *reflection* above moral *judgment*. It's crucial that we distinguish between these two kinds of moral reasoning as applied to historical study. Moral judgment, as I define it, is directed outward. It interrogates the past in order to draw conclusions about the individuals, groups, actions, or institutions that we encounter. Moral reflection, in contrast, is turned inward. It invites figures from the past to speak into *our* lives, to the end that we may more clearly see and more honestly evaluate our values, behavior, and worldview.

> **THE STUDY OF HISTORY AFFORDS A MARVELOUS FRAMEWORK FOR LIFE-CHANGING MORAL INQUIRY, PROVIDED THAT WE EMPHASIZE MORAL *REFLECTION* ABOVE MORAL *JUDGMENT*.**

As a Christian, I am leery of moral judgment because of its tendency to promote self-righteousness. As a historian, I oppose it for its tendency to shut down serious thought. Take the study of slavery in the nineteenth-century American South, for example. When we read fugitive-slave accounts such as *Narrative of the Life of Frederick Douglass* or *Incidents in the Life of a Slave Girl*, we're horrified by the accounts of brutality and exploitation that they contain, as we should be. When I say that we ought generally to avoid moral judgment, I am not suggesting that we respond to such episodes coldly or robotically. Because of our obligation to love those whom we encounter in the past, there will be times when our most appropriate response will be to "mourn with those who mourn" (Rom 12:15), grieving with those who lived their lives in chains.

The danger comes when we turn our attention from the enslaved to their masters. Here I think of Jesus' parable about the Pharisee and the tax collector who went into the temple to pray. According to Jesus, the Pharisee congratulated himself on his righteousness and prayed, "God, I thank you that I am not like other people." The tax collector was grieved by the darkness of his heart and pleaded, "God, have mercy on me, a sinner." Jesus explained that it was the tax collector who "went home justified before God. For all those who exalt themselves will be humbled, and those who humble themselves will be exalted" (Lk 18:9-14).

The serious study of history is always teaching us either humility or pride. We can't study the past for long without encountering individuals who did or said or believed things that we now hold to be immoral, even evil. And when that happens, our hearts and minds will lead us down one of two paths: toward self-exaltation—"God, I thank you that I am not like other people"—or toward a deeper awareness of our need for grace—"God, have mercy on me, a sinner."

Moral judgment in history inclines toward the first path. It's not just that we make moral pronouncements about a particular belief or practice from the past. We're tempted to dismiss its adherents as self-deceived sinners who, although we might not say so out loud, were worse people than we are. Not only does this externalize immorality—allowing us to condemn it without ever scrutinizing our own hearts—but it also tends to get in the way of our actually understanding the past. When we simply categorize slaveholders as evil, for example, we learn almost nothing about them. We just label them and move on, implicitly refusing to take their worldview seriously. Why pay attention to their testimony when we have already reached a verdict?

Moral reflection, on the other hand, consciously imitates the example of the tax collector. The starting point of moral reflection is "all have sinned and fall short of the glory of God," or even better, Paul's confession that "Christ Jesus came into the world to save sinners—of whom I am the worst" (Rom 3:23; 1 Tim 1:15).

> **MORAL REFLECTION MEANS THAT WE WORK TO *IDENTIFY* WITH THOSE WHOM WE ARE OTHERWISE TEMPTED TO JUDGE.**

In thinking about the past, this means that we work to *identify* with those whom we are otherwise tempted to judge. We acknowledge that their propensity to sin is no more developed than ours. In observing their moral struggles, we glimpse shadows of our own. When it comes to our encounter with Southern slaveholders, to continue with that example, we confront the likelihood that, had we been born into their cultural context, our attitudes and behavior would have looked a lot like theirs. This truth doesn't exonerate slaveholders, by the way. It implicates us.

In sum, one of the primary goals of moral reflection is to expose our hearts and, in the process, to "put our own lives to the test."[7] But because we know that we are finite as well as fallen, we also engage in moral reflection to invite the past to reveal our blind spots and remind us of forgotten truths. Here our starting point is not the tax collector's "have mercy on me, a sinner," but rather the humility of Job's friend Bildad, "We were born only yesterday and know nothing" (Job 8:9).

Two of the metaphors for history that we've already encountered can prove helpful in this latter regard. The first is the analogy, introduced in chapter four, of history as a kind of *mirror* that enables us to see in the present what might otherwise be invisible to us. When history functions in this role, we are in a better position to "take captive every thought to make it obedient to Christ" and resist the world's effort to squeeze us into its mold (2 Cor 10:5; see also Rom 12:2, Phillips).

To maximize this mirror-like function, I suggest that you *focus on the foreign in the past as much as the familiar.* Although the proportions will vary, the historical figures that we encounter always resemble us in some respects and differ from us in others. Our natural temptation, unfortunately, is to identify with what we see as familiar and stand in judgment over what we view as strange. We have to get over that if our study of history is to be truly educational.

---

[7] David Harlan, *The Degradation of American History* (Chicago: University of Chicago Press, 1997), xviii.

"We have no way of understanding where and who we are," Rowan Williams writes, "because we do not allow our ways of being and thinking to be made strange to us by the serious contemplation of other ways of being and thinking."[8] As Williams's lament suggests, it's the strangeness of the past that carries the greatest potential to challenge and change us, in large part because it's the strangeness of the past—not its more familiar aspects—that brings to light what we take for granted in the present.

> We have no way of understanding where and who we are, because we do not allow our ways of being and thinking to be made strange to us by the serious contemplation of other ways of being and thinking.
>
> Rowan Williams

The second metaphor that can facilitate moral reflection is the understanding of history as a form of conversation with the past that we discussed in chapter seven. Historian David Harlan observes that "at its best," the study of history "can be a conversation with the dead about what we should value and how we should live."[9] When we practice moral reflection, we enter into that conversation first of all through the hard work of *listening*—not just politely or condescendingly, as we might to an eccentric uncle at Christmastime, but with a commitment to truth and an

---

[8]Rowan Williams, *Why Study the Past?: The Quest for the Historical Church* (Grand Rapids: Eerdmans, 2005), 24.
[9]Harlan, *Degradation of American History*, xviii.

openness to learning *from* the past as well as *about* the past. This requires that we actively reject what C. S. Lewis called "chronological snobbery."[10] We listen to those who have gone before us without rolling our eyes, leaving open the possibility that something they have to say might be something we need to hear.

Sometimes figures from the past speak to us indirectly—hinting at their values and beliefs through the laws they enacted, the stories they told, the prayers they recorded, the wars they waged, the buildings they erected, the diaries they kept, even the epitaphs they inscribed. In other ways they speak to us directly, through their sermons and speeches and tracts and treatises full of explicit declarations about Permanent Things. I think of John Winthrop on board the *Arbella*, proclaiming that God has ordained that "in all times some must be rich, some poor, some high and eminent in power and dignity; others mean and in submission;" or James Madison during the struggle to ratify the US Constitution, warning that "if a majority be united by a common interest, the rights of the minority will be insecure;" or Alexis de Tocqueville, concluding after his tour of America that "despotism can do without faith, but liberty cannot."[11]

Whether they're direct or indirect, overt or implied, we must recognize these echoes from the past for what they are—an invitation to a dialogue across the ages about what it means

---

[10]C. S. Lewis, *Surprised by Joy* (New York: Harcourt, Brace, Jovanovich, 1966), 207-8.

[11]John Winthrop, "A Modell of Christian Charity," in *An American Primer,* ed. Daniel J. Boorstin (New York: Meridian, 1995), 28; James Madison, *Federalist* No. 51, in *The Federalist Papers,* ed. Clinton Rossiter (New York: Mentor, 1961), 323; Alexis de Tocqueville, *Democracy in America*, trans. Arthur Goldhammer (New York: Penguin Random House, 2004), 340.

to live wisely and well. But for that dialogue to be truly educational, we must do more than follow it and try to understand it. *We must bring the conversation into the present and respond to it personally.*

There is a difficult tension here. If we are to comprehend historical ideas and values accurately and fully, we must first situate them in their historical context (no context, no meaning). We must bring all of our critical faculties to bear in assessing the sources in which they are embedded, being careful to ask all of the questions about the author's identity and motive and audience and authority that we touched on in chapter seven. But at some point, we have to go further and *personalize* as well as contextualize our conversation with the past.

> AT SOME POINT, WE HAVE TO GO FURTHER AND *PERSONALIZE* AS WELL AS CONTEXTUALIZE OUR CONVERSATION WITH THE PAST.

And what does that mean? It means that when our conversation partners speak to us about "what we should value and how we should live," we refuse to move on without asking two simple questions. The first we pose to ourselves: "Is what I'm hearing *true*?" In today's postmodern academy, this is often the last question we think to ask, and yet it is imperative that we ask it if our encounter with the past is to be truly educational. If we are wise, we won't ask it in the spirit of moral judgment—rushing to condemn those with whom we disagree for their supposed blindness or arrogance or foolishness. Instead, we'll ask the question as a springboard to moral reflection and self-scrutiny. What do *I* believe and why? Nearly two centuries ago, Alexis de Tocqueville concluded that most of us fall into one of two categories with regard to our moral convictions: we will either "believe without knowing why, or not know precisely what [we] ought to believe."[12] If we're serious about "bringing every thought into captivity," we can't rest content in either state.

The second question, an invitation really, we pose to the past. As Beth Schweiger reminds us, it's "the question at the heart of Christian community, first posed by Christ to the disciples"—namely, "Tell me who you think I am."[13] It's a question we should pose to our conversation partners as well. Who do you think I am? What do you think I stand for? What are the values reflected in how I live? What do they reveal about what I love?

The book of Genesis tells how Jacob wrestled with God the whole night through, telling the Lord, "I will not let you go unless you bless me" (Gen 32:26). I can't begin to plumb the depths of that story's meaning, and yet I think of it often as I study the past. We should approach our study of the past with the expectation of blessing. "There will always be gifts to be received from the past," Rowan Williams says.[14] We must seek them persistently, tenaciously. If you're a new historian, you should expect to increase in historical knowledge, thinking skill,

---

[12]Tocqueville, *Democracy in America*, 213.

[13]Beth Barton Schweiger, "Seeing Things: Knowledge and Love in History," in *Confessing History: Explorations in Christian Faith and the Historian's Vocation,* ed. John Fea, Jay Green, and Eric Miller (Notre Dame: University of Notre Dame Press, 2010), 62.

[14]Williams, *Why Study the Past?*, 97.

and consciousness, but you should also hope to grow in humility, charity, and wisdom. The study of history, faithfully pursued, should alter your heart as well as your mind.

Don't settle for anything less.

What Is

References are to chapters of this book.

- History is *not* the past (chapter one).

- History *is*, among other things, the *recreation* of the past, the *analysis* or *interpretation* of the past, an *argument* about the past, or most broadly, the *remembered* past (chapter one).

- The analogy of history to memory leads to several key inferences (chapter one):

  - History is foundational to our sense of identity.

  - We all know some history.

  - We are all already historians.

  - (But) We are not automatically equipped to remember the past accurately and wisely.

- History is also an intellectual *discipline* in which the mind is trained to analyze historical evidence and build sound historical arguments (chapter one).

- Helpful *metaphors* for history include

  - history as *memory* (chapter one).

  - history as *mirror* (chapter four).

  - history as *conversation* (chapter six).

  - the historian as *host* or *hostess* (chapter seven).

  - the historian as *juror* (chapter seven).

WHAT IS THE CASE FOR THE IMPORTANCE OF HISTORY AND HISTORICAL STUDY?

- We are *historical beings*, creatures who live *in time*—our identity is rooted in the past, our very survival depends on memory of the past (chapter one, chapter three).

- Historical study changes what we know, how we think, and who we are, in part by increasing our

  - historical information: discrete facts about the past (chapter three);

  - historical understanding: a sense of how the facts fit together coherently (chapter three);

  - historical thinking skills: among others, the ability to read closely, think analytically, argue logically, and communicate persuasively (chapter three); and

  - historical consciousness: a mindset that changes how we see both ourselves and the world (chapter four).

- The intellectual skills that historical study sharpens are integral to any number of occupations (chapter three).

- Historical study equips us to be informed, responsible citizens (chapter three).

- Christians are *called* to be historians. The Christian case for the study of history rests on these pillars, among others (chapter five):

  - God *created* us to be historical beings.

  - History is absolutely foundational to Christianity.

  - Christians are members of a community of faith that binds living and dead, present and past.

  - Our faith informs us that the entire unfolding human story is worthy of attention.

  - In striving to understand the past, we stand on holy ground.

  - Historical understanding plays a vital role in faithful Christian discipleship.

PRINCIPLES FOR STUDYING HISTORY FAITHFULLY

- In engaging secondary sources, strive to (chapter six)

  - cultivate epistemological humility—be conscious of your limited ability to know the past.

  - take the metaphor of *conversation* seriously—you are entering into a highly *interpretive* conversation *about* the past, not watching as the past "comes alive."

  - get to know your conversation partner—find out what "bees he has in his bonnet."

- • focus on interpretation first, facts second—the facts mean nothing apart from the author's larger interpretation.

- • think long term—in the long run you will forget most of the discrete facts; how are your historical understanding and consciousness being altered?

- In engaging primary sources, strive to (chapter seven)

  - • actively *love* the human beings reflected in the sources— notice them, listen carefully to them, respect their perspective, and be open to learning from them.

  - • practice *discernment* by critically assessing their trustworthiness—situate the source in its larger historical context; determine the author's identity, motive, audience, and authority; and search for external corroboration.

  - • approach them with *humility*, disciplining your mind to doubt your natural ability to understand historical evidence—combat presentism by avoiding snap judgments and "cultivating puzzlement."

- When undertaking your own research project (chapter eight),

  - • practice metacognition all along the way—be as self-conscious as you can in thinking about how you are thinking as you proceed. A research project affords a wonderful opportunity both to apply and to reinforce historical habits of mind.

  - • consciously enter into *two* kinds of conversation—an effective history paper listens to the dead in order to speak to the living.

- be mindful that the evidence won't speak for itself—you must contribute your own interpretation of the evidence, which makes writing an effective history paper an act of creating as much as discovering.

- pay constant attention to the "five C's of historical thinking": change over time, context, causality, contingency, and complexity.

- To make historical study part of a larger quest for wisdom (chapter nine),

    - train your mind to expect life-changing insight, and be proactive in seeking it.

    - keep in mind that the proper focus of historical research is human beings, not God.

    - emphasize moral *reflection* (which is directed inward) above moral *judgment* (which is directed outward).

    - focus on the foreign in the past as much as the familiar—it's the strangeness of the past that carries the greatest potential to challenge and change us.

    - bring the historical conversation you are engaging in into the present and respond to it personally. Ask yourself, "Is what I am hearing true?" and invite your historical neighbor to "tell me who you think I am."

GENERAL INDEX

SCRIPTURE INDEX

LITTLE BOOKS SERIES

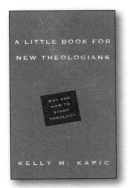

**A LITTLE BOOK FOR
NEW THEOLOGIANS**

Kelly M. Kapic

**A LITTLE BOOK FOR
NEW SCIENTISTS**

Josh A. Reeves & Steve Donaldson

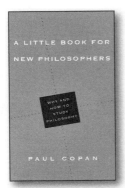

**A LITTLE BOOK FOR
NEW PHILOSOPHERS**

Paul Copan

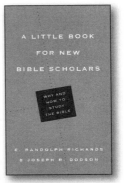

**A LITTLE BOOK FOR
NEW BIBLE SCHOLARS**

*E. Randolph Richards
& Joseph R. Dodson*

Finding the Textbook You Need

The IVP Academic Textbook Selector
is an online tool for instantly finding the IVP books
suitable for over 250 courses across 24 disciplines.

---

ivpacademic.com
